T0318883

Cambridge Elements ☰

Elements in the Global Middle Ages
edited by
Geraldine Heng
University of Texas at Austin
Susan Noakes
University of Minnesota, Twin Cities

MEDIEVAL TEXTILES ACROSS EURASIA, C. 300–1400

Patricia Blessing
Princeton University

Elizabeth Dospěl Williams
Dumbarton Oaks

Eiren L. Shea
Grinnell College

CAMBRIDGE
UNIVERSITY PRESS

CAMBRIDGE
UNIVERSITY PRESS

Shaftesbury Road, Cambridge CB2 8EA, United Kingdom

One Liberty Plaza, 20th Floor, New York, NY 10006, USA

477 Williamstown Road, Port Melbourne, VIC 3207, Australia

314–321, 3rd Floor, Plot 3, Splendor Forum, Jasola District Centre,
New Delhi – 110025, India

103 Penang Road, #05–06/07, Visioncrest Commercial, Singapore 238467

Cambridge University Press is part of Cambridge University Press & Assessment,
a department of the University of Cambridge.

We share the University's mission to contribute to society through the pursuit of
education, learning and research at the highest international levels of excellence.

www.cambridge.org
Information on this title: www.cambridge.org/9781009393362

DOI: 10.1017/9781009393379

First published 2023

A catalogue record for this publication is available from the British Library.

ISBN 978-1-009-39336-2 Paperback
ISSN 2632-3427 (online)
ISSN 2632-3419 (print)

Medieval Textiles across Eurasia, c. 300–1400

Elements in the Global Middle Ages

DOI: 10.1017/9781009393379
First published online: May 2023

Patricia Blessing
Princeton University

Elizabeth Dospěl Williams
Dumbarton Oaks

Eiren L. Shea
Grinnell College

Author for correspondence: Patricia Blessing, pblessing@princeton.edu

Abstract: This Element considers the textiles made, traded, and exchanged across Eurasia from late antiquity to the late Middle Ages with special attention to the sociopolitical and cultural aspects of this universal medium. It presents a wide range of textiles used in both sacred and secular settings, as dress and furnishings, and for elite and ordinary owners. The introduction presents historiographical background to the study of textiles and explains the conditions of their survival in archaeological contexts and museums. A section on the materials and techniques used to produce textiles is followed by those outlining textile production, industry, and trade across Eurasia. Further sections examine the uses for dress and furnishing textiles and the appearance of imported fabrics in European contexts, addressing textiles' functions and uses in medieval societies. Finally, a concluding section on textile aesthetics connects fabrics to their broader visual and material context.

Keywords: textiles, dress, costume history, medieval Eurasia, weaving techniques

ISBNs: 9781009393362 (PB), 9781009393379 (OC)
ISSNs: 2632-3427 (online), 2632-3419 (print)

Contents

1 Introduction

This Element introduces the reader to the rich world of textiles made, traded, and exchanged across Eurasia from late antiquity to the late Middle Ages. With its geographical span reaching from Europe across the Middle East and Central Asia into China, the volume presents a wide range of textiles that were made for many uses, both sacred and secular, as dress and furnishings, for elite and ordinary owners. We do not assume any previous knowledge of textiles on the part of readers. Rather, we present a general introduction for those who find late antique and medieval textiles interesting, compelling, and beautiful, but may have found themselves intimidated by the myriad technical details of specialist publications written by and for textile historians. While all three of us have written and engaged with such academic work, we have written and imagined this study with the premise that textiles should and can be an approachable, ubiquitous medium for scholars, students, and the general public. Drawing from a multidisciplinary perspective, we encourage readers to explore further in a more specialized Bibliography included at the end of the Element. Readers will find full-color photographs in the online and e-book version of this Element.

The scope of this Element is defined, on the one hand, by our combined set of expertise and, on the other hand, by what materials have been photographed and published, particularly those made accessible online. This latter aspect has become pressing as we were researching and writing this Element during the global Covid-19 pandemic beginning in spring 2020, and had limited access to library resources or museum objects, apart from what all three of us had in hand from earlier projects or could access digitally. These challenges continued as libraries began to reopen, and travel remains difficult as we complete this Element in December 2021 and revise it in September 2022. Furthermore, we acknowledge that textiles have been produced around the globe for nearly as long as humans have needed clothing, and that neither the geographical nor chronological scope of this volume provides a fully global history of textiles. That task would require a much longer publication, and a team of close to ten authors. Hopefully, additional Elements exploring textiles in Southeast Asia, sub-Saharan Africa, the Americas, and Oceania can be added to the series in the future.

We focus on textiles made in major centers in the Byzantine Empire, the Islamic world, and China. These regions were producing textiles at a large scale early on, ranging from linen tunics and shrouds to silk fabrics interwoven with gold and silver. For much of the period under investigation, Europe was on the receiving end of transregional textile trade: luxury textiles produced elsewhere were imported, coveted for court dress and ecclesiastical use. The latter explains why many Byzantine, Islamic, Central Asian, and Chinese textiles have been preserved in European churches. Used for liturgical garments and as wrappings for saints' relics, and carefully tucked away in shrines, many such textiles were preserved for centuries.

Our Element starts with a general discussion of materials and techniques used to produce textiles, a recognition that this approach has long dominated scholarship on these materials. We then move on to consider the organization of the textile industry and questions about trade. Sections on the functions of textiles focus on dress and furnishing textiles, as well as the appearance of imported textiles in Europe. Lastly, our section on the textile aesthetics connects fabrics to their broader visual and material contexts. Overall, we present an easily accessible introduction to the history of textiles in medieval Eurasia that includes production, trade, and function alongside the various roles that fabrics played in people's lives.

Attention to both sociohistorical context and technical details are a central aspect of the Element. In addition to a separate section on technical and material aspects, these topics will also be explained alongside objects' functions and meanings. We contend that materials and technique — from sourcing fibers to spinning, dyeing, weaving, and finally sewing — is a crucial aspect of textile history. Yet readers find those discussions often most intimidating, and students tend to shy away from purely technical discussions, unless they have worked with textiles themselves. Integrating technical aspects with the overall discussion of each example, therefore, will allow readers to engage with these perhaps daunting aspects together with more familiar terrain, such as how garments were worn or how textiles were used to furnish rooms.

The discussion of different fibers — cotton, linen, silk, wool — also introduces patterns of agricultural production and trade as at times, raw materials rather than finished textiles were moved between regions. For instance, silk produced in Northern Iran was imported to the Ottoman Empire at least until the early sixteenth century. Dyestuffs could be sourced from locally available plants and animals, or had to be imported across wide-reaching trade networks. Precious textiles were gifts from rulers to courtiers and allies alike. Large-scale professional workshops produced fabrics, but so did women who worked at home or in groups, both for domestic use and to sell at a smaller scale. Thus, textiles carry not only the histories of their users and wearers but also of their makers, and offer insights in the gender and class dynamics of the premodern period.

The textiles we present have survived to us today thanks to a variety of circumstances, including as grave goods and relic wrappings. It is therefore impossible to discuss medieval textiles without also acknowledging the ways in which these textiles came to light. Often, they were cut up by dealers who wished to render fragments more aesthetically pleasing (Thomas 2009 on Byzantine textiles; Blessing 2022 for Islamic textiles in this context). Many were transferred to various museums in the nineteenth century, where they were catalogued according to perceived cultural origins without much regard for the often confounding overlap in styles, structures, materials, and the rich evidence for their widespread movement through trade. The loss of contextual information following these interventions creates ongoing challenges to our research. It also helps explain why so much scholarship has for so long focused on attributing textiles to places of production rather than considering their uses and reuses in the medieval period. In this sense, studying medieval textiles today necessitates a discussion of collecting practices, and the ways in which textile preservation and restoration have developed over the last century, a theme that will also carry through this Element.

Even within archaeological contexts, a further challenge is that textiles are rarely preserved in situ, and if so, have often deteriorated significantly, for instance when they were used in funerary contexts. Because such textiles undergo chemical changes, no amount of restoration can return them to their original states (Harris 2019). This is for instance the case for late antique and medieval textiles found in burials of Christians and Muslims in Egypt (Sokoly 1997). When such textiles entered museum collections in the nineteenth and early twentieth centuries, they were cut apart and even at times washed to remove the remnants of the human bodies they were buried with (McWilliams and Sokoly 2022).

What is more difficult to understand within archaeological contexts is how people used textiles and interacted with them in their daily lives. New approaches in sensory archaeology aim at reconstructing such experiences in which textiles are seen as sensory objects to which humans react with several senses at once (Harris 2019). To better comprehend this, consider a piece of clothing that you are wearing. You feel its weight and texture on your skin, you hear its sounds when you move, you see its color and the sheen of its fibers, and you smell the lingering scent of laundry detergent. And yet, it is these very sensory properties of textiles that break down over time, especially if buried in the ground. Furthermore, textiles can also change sensory interactions with the objects and bodies they wrap. Humans' interactions with textiles, and their reactions to them, change over time and are also culturally conditioned (Harris 2019). Therefore, we should not presume that our contemporary reaction to a textile is identical to that of the individual(s) who used it in the past. In the present day, we often view textiles as simply utilitarian, to the point of barely registering the large role they play in our daily lives. Just looking around one's dining room, one might see placemats on the table, a child's toys on the floor, coats, tote bags, and umbrellas hanging on hooks in the hallway. One might become aware of the clothing that one is wearing. These objects might register more clearly as textiles while writing a text such as the one in hand. On another day, one might not think much about these items. By and large, these textiles are ones of daily use that serve to protect our bodies, or to carry and cover practical objects such as books and tables, and that we take for granted as being present in our households. Such functions are of course also part of historical uses of textiles, and we will include, for instance, clothing and furnishing textiles to the extent that they have survived. At the same time, there are multiple symbolic uses of textiles, from canopies over royal thrones to wrappings for relics, that will also be addressed.

2 Materials and Techniques

Studies on materials and techniques have long dominated scholarship on medieval textiles, often serving as a baseline for further investigation (Colburn 2012; De Moor et al. 2015; Krody 2019; Kuhn and Zhao 2012; Mackie 2015). Since scholars often had little contextual information to go on, focusing on textiles' technical details offered important evidence for attribution and dating of works. Interest in materials and techniques also grew from a particular branch of art historical scholarship concerned with craft and decorative arts and its intersection with the development of the European textile industry in the modern era (Fulghum 2001–02; Thomas 2009; Walker 2012). For example, major collections of textiles in European collections, such as the Victoria and Albert Museum in London, were built to inspire contemporary textile producers to study the structures and materials of medieval textiles as inspiration for modern ones (Calament 2005; Hoskins 2004).

Vocabulary and terminology are hotly debated in ancient and medieval textile scholarship. Although the Centre International d'Etudes des Textiles Anciens (CIETA) is widely recognized as the standard-bearer for defining and translating textile terms in a variety of European languages, there are in reality no objective standards for describing often related yet distinctive aspects in the structural qualities, raw materials, and manufacture of fabrics (Burnham 1980; CIETA 2006; Phipps 2011). Furthermore, it is useful upfront to define what we mean by "material" and "technique," as these terms have specific resonances in textile scholarship. "Materials" encompass the raw resources for threads, such as fibers and dyes. Fibers like **linen** (flax) and **cotton**, for example, are sourced from plants and their physical properties resulted in absorbent threads excellent for lightweight fabrics (Lamm 1937). Animal hair, such as **wool**, is crisper, denser, and absorbs dyes well, making this material excellent for colorful, heavy, and warm weavings. The cocoons of silkworms are spun from single threads that produce innately strong, smooth, and lustrous fibers, properties uniquely admired in **silk** weaving (sericulture). Threads are prepared in a variety of manners depending on the desired quality of the cloth. Yarns can be twisted clockwise or counterclockwise to produce spun thread, sometimes referred to as **S- or Z-twist** depending on the direction of the spin. The tightness of the spin and the thickness of the fiber can be manipulated to create fuzzy, loose, thick threads or tightly spun, thin ones. Weavers can introduce additional reinforcement and create thicker threads by twisting single threads together to create **plied threads**.

Much research into medieval textile dyes is the result of individual case studies that have not been fully synthesized to reflect this rapidly developing field of research (Cardon 2007; Kirby 2014). Both finished textiles and individual threads could be left undyed or prepared in a range of colors through various chemical processes. Scientific analyses can identify **dyes**, **mordants**, and other chemical preparations used to create the range of colors we see in medieval textiles today. **Dyestuffs** like woad, weld, madder, and indigo, for example, were derived from plants; lac and cochineal were sourced from insect shells; and murex from mollusk shells (Balfour-Paul 1997; Donkin 1977; Susmann 2020; Wertz et al. 2022; Wouters 1995). These dyes could be mixed and prepared with various mordants, such as alum, to produce a range of color tonalities. Threads were sometimes enhanced with precious metals, as well: gold leaf could be applied with resin or glue on top finished fabrics, while silver and gold were sometimes flattened into wires and wrapped around threads and woven into the fabric's structure (Figure 1).

Today, scientific analyses are the only reliable way to identify the colors of medieval fabrics. Sophisticated medieval weavers mixed pigments and mordants in varying degrees, sometimes to produce what visually appears to be the same color with different chemical properties. Some pigments decay over time, so that the present-day visual appearance does often not reflect what textiles

Figure 1 Neck ornament found in Egypt. Late antique period, third–fourth century (?). Medium/technique: Wool, linen, and gold-wrapped silk thread slit tapestry. Dimensions: Overall – 56.9 × 15.8 cm (22 3/8 × 6 1/4 in.). Museum of Fine Arts, Boston, Charles Potter Kling Fund, accession number 46.401. Photograph © 2023 Museum of Fine Arts, Boston.

would have looked like originally (Houghteling 2020). This is why dye analysis is crucial, and can advance our knowledge about dating textiles, together with radiocarbon (C-14) dating (Cabrera Lafuente 2020).

"Technique" is best understood as the weaving process; the finished fabric is the result of a weaving technique, or sometimes multiple techniques. A textile's structure is evidence of technique, but it is not necessarily the technique itself, a point central to Irene Emery's essential encyclopedia of weave structures (Emery 2009). Though the weave structures Emery describes in her book appear in textiles from around the world and across time, the techniques that produced those structures were culturally specific. One might find the exact same plain-weave structure in textiles from Peru and from Egypt produced at the same time, for example, but the processes behind those structures — the technique — may have been different. The distinction is important when discussing textiles produced in different geographic locales that may have been the result of culturally and period-specific techniques.

Still, in much scholarship on medieval textiles, "technique" and structure are often described interchangeably, because the fabrics themselves are often all that remain to tell us today about their processes of production. **Warps** are threads that support the fabric's structure and define its overall size and proportions. **Wefts** are the threads that run over the warp, filling in these spaces and creating a surface-facing pattern. **Plain weave** (sometimes called **tabby weave**) represents the most easily recognizable structure: a one-to-one relationship of a warp and weft resembling a grid (Figure 2). **Pile weave** such as velvet featured looped tufts of weft (sometimes warp) pulled through a plain-weave ground, producing a densely cushioned, plush fabric. Such loops could be spliced, producing a cut pile; conversely, weavers could insert and tie individual threads in the plain-weave ground, resulting in a knotted pile. These techniques provided additional heft, stiffness, and weight that made such fabrics suitable for floor coverings and bedding (Figure 3). **Felt**, in contrast, was not woven, but was rather created by condensing or pressing wet fibers together to produce the fabric's structure. The finished edges of a textile, the **selvedges**, provide an important diagnostic to understand the dimensions of pieces in fragmentary condition today.

Tapestry weave builds on the basic relationship of warp and weft by playing with the density of the threads to create fields of color and patterns in the fabric's structure, akin to blotches of paint on the surface of a canvas (Figure 4 and Figure 5). Although in popular usage today, the term connotes large-format furnishing hangings in this technique (like the Unicorn Tapestries)[1]; in reality, tapestry was used for all types of textiles, especially in the

---

[1] www.metmuseum.org/art/collection/search/467642.

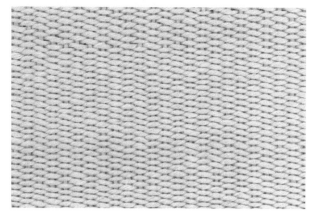

Figure 2 Weft-faced plain weave, after Irene Emery. Photograph by Pam Kaplan, © The George Washington University Museum and The Textile Museum.

Figure 3 Carpet fragment with mosaic floor pattern, said to be from Egypt, Antinoöpolis. Fourth–fifth century. Medium/technique: Wool (warp, weft and pile); symmetrically knotted pile. Dimensions: Rug – L. 102 cm (40 3/16 in.) × W. 117 cm (46 1 1/6 in.). Metropolitan Museum of Art, New York, Rogers Fund, 1931, accession number: 31.2.1. Open access CC0.

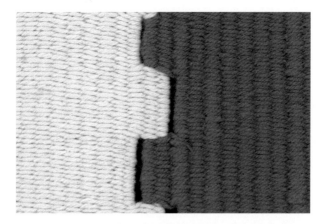

Figure 4 Tapestry weave, after Irene Emery. Photograph by Pam Kaplan, © The George Washington University Museum and The Textile Museum.

Figure 5 Fragment of a hanging or cover with head and duck in jeweled lattice from Egypt. First-third of fifth century. Dimensions: H. (warp) 33.0 cm × W. (weft) 22.0 cm (13 × 8 11/16 in.). Medium/technique: Tapestry weave in polychrome wool. © Byzantine Collection, Dumbarton Oaks Research Library and Collection, Washington, DC, BZ. 1946.16.

Figure 6 Textile fragment, fifth century, attributed to Egypt. Medium: Wool, linen; plain weave, weft-loop weave. Dimensions: Max. H. 165 cm (64 15/16 in.) × max. W. 128.4 cm (50 9/16 in.). Metropolitan Museum of Art, New York, Gift of George F. Baker, 1890, accession number: 90.5.808. Open access CC0.

late antique period, including dress textiles. The combination of plain weave, tapestry weave, and sometimes even weft-loop pile was also common, as one sees often in weavings from late antique Egypt (Figure 6). Plain weave was useful when one needed to create a large-format utilitarian garment or hanging, because the resulting fabric was lightweight and used relatively little thread; denser-woven tapestry areas were better for decorative details and to create heft (Colburn 2019).

Plain weave and tapestry are categorized as simple weave structures in that they are essentially variations on the basic arrangement of warp and weft. Over the course of the Middle Ages, however, increasingly advanced looms resulted in ever more sophisticated structures, known as **complex** or **compound weaves** (Mackie 2015: 469–470). Scholars continue to debate the techniques used to make these structurally sophisticated weavings and the locations of their production across Eurasia. Silks are perhaps the best and most studied of medieval compound weaves (Galliker 2015b; Kuhn and Zhao 2012; Muthesius 1997; Thomas 2012). While plain weave and tapestry weave could be completed on a relatively simple loom with patterns introduced by hand, compound silk fabrics

were woven on a drawloom, a large, mechanized weaving machine that introduced repetition into the weaving process (Muthesius 1997: 19–27; Zhao et al.
2019). In the earliest examples, patterns were programmed into the loom, which
then repeated and mirrored these patterns across a run of fabric, with the resulting
basic structure, sometimes called **samite** (weft-faced compound twill), creating
a front and back of the textile in reversed colors (Figure 7). The number of colors
used and the size of the individual repeat unit reflected the complexity of the loom
used for the weaving; silks with large-format medallions and multiple colors were
among the most technologically advanced artistic products of the Middle Ages.
Silk technology originated in China before spreading to Central Asia and into
Byzantium; by the sixth century, silk production was common in the
Mediterranean basin with production centers in Egypt and the Levant.

Figure 7 "Hero and lion" silk. Constantinople? Egypt? Syria? Seventh–ninth
century. Dimensions: H. 94.2 × W. 38.4 cm (37 1/16 × 15 1/8 in.). Technique/
material: Weft-faced compound twill (samite) in polychrome silk. © Byzantine
Collection, Dumbarton Oaks Research Library and Collection, Washington,
DC, BZ.1934.1.

In the later Middle Ages, a range of compound weaves emerged throughout the Middle East and Europe as technologies from East and Central Asia spread West (Mackie 1984; Mackie 2015: 211–239). Textiles in these later centuries featured increasingly customized and complex warp and weft structures, sometimes combining elements of different techniques. **Satin damask** (Figure 8), first woven in southern China in the first half of the fourteenth century, quickly spread into the Mediterranean by the end of the century and could be woven on the same looms used to create some forms of samite (Shea 2021a). Unpatterned satin weave, now considered alongside plain weave (tabby) and twill to be one of the three principal weaves, developed from the technique of satin damask. **Double cloth**, seen in Fatimid- and Mamluk-era textiles, featured two intersecting plain weaves, producing different patterns on the front and back of the textile (Figure 9). **Lampas** and **taqueté** were silk weaving techniques deploying multiple warp and weft systems to create colorful and structurally complex textiles with a range of decorative and patterning possibilities (Figure 10 and Figure 11). By the fourteenth century, lampas and taqueté were found in textiles produced all over Europe and the Middle East, but with particular sophistication in Egypt, Italy, and Spain. In Central Asia, the Mongols promoted an exceptional compound weave known as *nasij* or "cloth of gold" (Figures 10, 11, and 12) made of silk and precious gold-wrapped threads (Monnas 2008; Mühlemann 2017). Local emulations of luxury textiles suggest not only the movement of finished goods but also of industrial technology and craftspeople who brought knowledge of these weaving techniques with them.

Figure 8 Damask with cloud palmettes and Chinese characters. China, Yuan dynasty (1271–1368). Fourteenth century. Medium: Silk satin damask. Dimensions: Overall – 27.9 × 21.6 cm (11 × 8 1/2 in.). Mount: 38.1 × 31.7 × 3.8 cm (15 × 12 1/2 × 1 1/2 in.). Metropolitan Museum of Art, New York, Fletcher Fund, 1946, accession number: 46.156.20. Open access CC0.

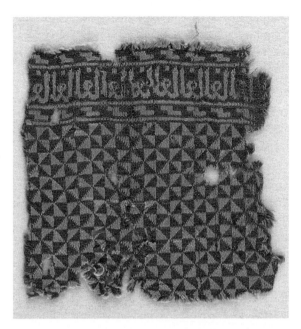

Figure 9 Fragment. 800–1150, Egypt, Fatimid period. Double cloth. Dimensions: Overall – 0.5 × 10.5 cm (4 1/8 × 4 1/8 in.). The Textile Museum Collection, Washington, DC, Museum Purchase, 1961.22.15. Open access CC0.

Finished weavings could be embellished in a range of techniques adding visual interest to the fabric's structure, rather than integrally woven into the fabric itself. In **block printing** and **resist-dying** techniques, weavers imprinted and drew colorful patterns on plain-weave fabrics, sometimes using multiple dyeing processes to introduce a range of colors to the finished fabric (Figure 13). Block-printed and resist-dyed textiles (Figure 14) were a specialty of the Gujarat region in India, and surviving examples and emulations in late Roman, Byzantine, and Islamic Egypt attest to the particular popularity of these textiles there, thanks to a vibrant trade along the Red Sea (Barnes 1997; Rosenfeld 2016).

In the Islamic period, simple plain-weave fabrics were woven with individually dyed threads that created blurred patterns, a sophisticated technique both decorative and structural known as **ikat** (Figure 15). **Brocade**, an ornamental technique where supplementary threads were integrated in a fabric's surface structure could be used to add visual and textual interest, sometimes quite spectacularly as in the case of luxury textiles embellished further with

Figure 10 Cloth of gold with winged lions and griffins, 1225–75, Central Asia. Silk and gold thread: lampas. Dimensions: Overall – 124 × 48.8 cm (48 13/16 × 19 3/16 in.). Cleveland Museum of Art, Cleveland, purchase from the J. H. Wade Fund, 1989.50. Open access CC0.

brocading details (see Figures 32 and 33). **Embroidery**, another supplementary technique where thread was added to a fabric's finished surface for decorative effect, can be found in textiles produced throughout Asia, the Middle East, and Europe throughout the Middle Ages. In the Islamic world, prized **tiraz**, or textiles inscribed in Arabic, are believed to have developed out of traditions of embroidering words on fabrics in the Persianate sphere (Figure 16). Metal threads were an especially popular choice for embroidery; the inherent value of the precious metals used for such threads meant they were used sparingly (Figure 17). Perhaps the most famous medieval fabric of all, the Bayeux Tapestry is in fact a masterpiece of embroidery.[2] The technique developed

---

[2] www.bayeuxmuseum.com/en/the-bayeux-tapestry/discover-the-bayeux-tapestry/explore-online/.

Figure 11 Dalmatic with motifs of pelicans and cows. Fourteenth century, textile woven in Iran, tailored into a dalmatic in Germany. Material: Silk and gilt metal thread: lampas. Dimensions: Overall – 171.5 × 121.92 cm (67 1/2 × 48 in.) Victoria and Albert Museum, London, 8361–1863.

Figure 12 Dragons chasing flaming pearls by unidentified artist. Chinese. Fourteenth century. Yuan dynasty (1271–1368). Medium: Silk lampas with supplementary metal thread wefts. Dimensions: Overall – 22 × 27.5 cm (8 11/16 × 10 13/16 in.). Metropolitan Museum of Art, New York, Gift of Robert D. Mowry, in honor of Claudia Brown and in memory of Donald N. Rabiner, 2020, accession number: 2020.78. Open access CC0.

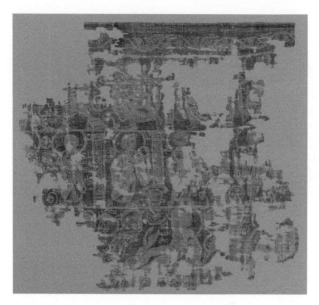

Figure 13 Resist-dyed hanging with biblical scenes, 500–550, Egypt. Resist-dyed linen; plain weave. Dimensions: Overall – 99.7 × 104.8 cm (39 1/4 × 41 1/4 in.). Mounted: 111.1 × 114.3 × 2.5 cm (43 3/4 × 45 × 1 in.). Cleveland Museum of Art, Cleveland, John L. Severance Fund, 1951.400. Open access CC0.

Figure 14 Hanging decorated with crosses and floral motifs, fifth–seventh century, Ancient and Byzantine world, Africa, Bawit (Egypt). Harvard Art Museums Hagop Kevorkian Foundation, 1975.41.31. Photograph © President and Fellows of Harvard College.

Figure 15 Ikat fragments with inscription. Yemen, later tenth century.
Dimensions: H. 33.3 cm × W. 55.3 cm (13 1/8 × 21 3/4 in.). Medium/technique:
Gold paint and ink on warp-faced plain-woven cotton ikat.
© Byzantine Collection, Dumbarton Oaks Research Library and Collection,
Washington, DC, BZ.1933.37.

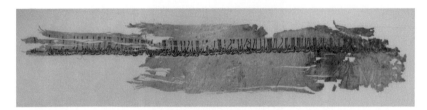

Figure 16 Fragment of mulham tiraz naming al-Qadir bi-Allah. Iraq,
1008/1009 (399 AH). Dimensions: H. 8.7 cm × W. 48.3 cm (3 7/16 × 19
in.). Medium/technique: Weft-faced plain weave (cotton warp, silk weft)
with chain-stitched embroidery in silk.
© Byzantine Collection, Dumbarton Oaks Research Library and
Collection, Washington, DC, BZ.1933.22.

Figure 17 Fragment with mythological animals in roundels, Mesopotamian (possibly Baghdad), tenth–eleventh century. Medium/technique: Silk and cotton plain weave (mulham), embroidered with silk and metal-wrapped thread. Dimensions: Overall – 68.5 × 50.5 cm (26 15/16 × 19 7/8 in.). Museum of Fine Arts, Boston, Archibald Cary Coolidge Fund, accession number 37.103. Photograph © 2023 Museum of Fine Arts, Boston.

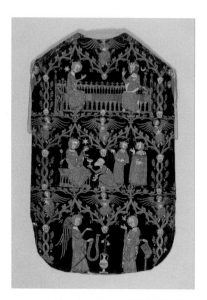

Figure 18 Chasuble (opus anglicanum), ca. 1330–50, England. Medium: Silver and silver-gilt thread and colored silks in underside couching, split stitch, laid-and-couched work, and raised work, with pearls on velvet. Dimensions: Overall – (chasuble): 129.5 × 76.2 cm (51 × 30 in.). Fletcher Fund, 1927. Metropolitan Museum of Art, New York, accession number: 27.162.1. Open access CC0.

with particular sophistication in late medieval England, where it was known (in Latin) as **opus anglicanum** (Figure 18), that is, English work.[3]

3 Industry

In many places across Eurasia in the period between 300 and 1400, weaving was women's work. Women seem almost universally to have been charged with clothing their families and their homes (Garver 2018). Women prepared raw materials, spun thread, wove cloth, sewed clothing, and also created much of the textile landscape of the home — textiles used for bedding or the table, for example. In some places, wealthier households could buy lengths of finer cloth at markets. Cloth sold at market was often produced in small household workshops. Certain elite households also employed their own weavers and tailors, and elite women in medieval Europe often worked on embroideries (Gajewski and Seeberg 2016). Alongside household workshops, many palaces had central government or royal workshops to produce the textiles required by court officials, royals, and members of the clergy.

3.1 Weavers and Workshop Practices

In China, women were explicitly connected to silk production (sericulture) and the weaving of the silk into cloth from the first millennium BCE – this gendered association continued until the twentieth century (Kuhn and Zhao 2012). However, we know from historical texts that both men and women wove textiles from an early period. For example, in the Western Han dynasty during the reign of Emperor Wudi (r. 141–87 BCE), thousands of men and women were employed as weavers in the Three Seasons Tailoring Workshop (*sanfuguan*), an imperial workshop located in present-day Shandong Province that wove clothing for the court (Li in Kuhn and Zhao 2012). Nonetheless, women were broadly associated with both the production and weaving of silk. This was manifested both in the actual production of raw silk and silk cloth, and in legends and rituals. For example, sacrificing at the altar of the first sericulturist, Xiling or Lady Leizu (the wife of the legendary Yellow Emperor), became a duty of the empress at least by the third century CE, and continued through the centuries between 300 and 1400 (Kuhn 1984). Another well-known story, the legend of the Chinese Silk Princess, recorded by the pilgrim monk Xuanzang in the seventh century, also exemplifies the connection between women and silk making

---

[3] www.vam.ac.uk/exhibitions/opus-anglicanum-masterpieces-of-english-medieval-embroidery.

(Li 1996). In this tale, a Chinese princess living in the mid-fifth century and betrothed to the King of Khotan (an oasis town at the edge of the Taklamakan desert) is told by the envoy of the Khotanese king that there is no way to make silk in Khotan as there are no silkworms or mulberry trees. Alarmed, the princess decides to smuggle mulberry seeds and silk-worm eggs in her headdress, which she knows will not be searched by the border guards, thus assuring the production of silk in her new home.

In Japan, too, women were associated with silk production. The Nara period (710–784) saw the introduction of many cultural practices from Tang China, including rituals linked to sericulture. Weaving and sericulture were explicitly connected to women's work, and as in China, the empress played a primary role in courtly rituals surrounding sericulture and weaving (Como 2005). In the Heian period (794–1185), the Bureau of the Wardrobe (*nuidonoryō*, "Bureau of Needlework") was headed by a high-level male official and produced clothing for the imperial family and for elite partici-pants in special courtly ceremonies. However, Office of the Imperial Wardrobe, a parallel office which eventually took over much of the produc-tion of court dress from the Bureau of the Wardrobe, was headed by a woman, the Keeper of the Robes (Dusenbury 2015). Elite women also staffed the Bureau of the Wardrobe. In Byzantium, both men and women were involved in the production of silk, with stages of silk production — such as preparing yarns, dyeing, and weaving — happening in private domestic contexts as well as imperial and private workshops (Galliker 2015a: 132–134; Lopez 1945; Maniatis 1999).

3.2 Technology and Places of Production

As is evident from the central place sericulture and silk weaving had in Chinese society, silk was the most widely manufactured textile in China, although textiles made from hemp and wool also existed. Many of the textiles that we consider in this Element are made of silk. Silk production, or sericulture, originated in China in the first millennium BCE, and raw and woven silks began to be traded from China with peoples in Central Asia by the second century BCE following the mission to Central Asia headed by the Chinese envoy Zhang Qian (Liu 2010). Indeed, the desire that Central Asians, Persians, and Romans had for Chinese silk was at the origins of the trans-Asian trade routes named the Silk Road (Seidenstraße) in the nineteenth century by Ferdinand von Richthofen. The ability to weave raw silk and sericulture itself spread gradually west into Central Asia, West Asia, and the Eastern Mediterranean, including Byzantium, from the third through eighth centuries through trade, but also through the displacement of textile workers, who brought their knowledge of sericulture and silk weaving with them (Woodward Wendleken 2014). However, a major challenge in discerning changes in textile production (silk and otherwise) in the late Roman and Byzantine Mediterranean is the uneven nature of the evidence. Archaeological evidence for production — such as looms and workshops — is scarce (Carroll 1998). Surviving tools found in domestic settings support the idea that at least some stages of textile production, such as the processing of raw materials, took place at home, likely as a cottage industry. The survival of loom posts in monks' cells in Egypt suggest that some production did occur there, though whether monks wove humble fabrics for use within the monastery or more sophisticated cloth for trade remains unclear (Sigl 2020).

A rich corpus of Greek, Coptic, and Arabic texts preserved on fragmentary papyri and ostraka (potsherds), however, offers precious insight into the conditions of the textile industry within Egypt and beyond. These sources are usually studied by papyrologists within a broader context of economic history, especially taxation and trade (Kelley 2019; Wipszycka 1965). Tax receipts record the movement of raw materials like cotton and plant fibers from rural agricultural areas to trade emporia for further processing. Receipts, inventories, and wills at times describe finished tunics or furnishing fabrics, at times even with valuations. Letters record the activities of weavers, including practices of consigning children and teenagers to apprenticeships. A major stumbling block to analyzing these deep reserves of evidence, however, is the challenge of linking technical terminology in written sources to extant archaeological textiles. Papyrologists and art historians bridging these fields are increasingly attentive to methodological concerns (Bogensperger 2016). Of particular ongoing interest are unresolved questions about the gender of weavers, dyers, and other textile workers in the late antique and Byzantine Mediterranean, as well as the role of unfree labor and enslaved people in textile production (Kelley 2022).

The study of pattern sheets sits precisely at the crossroads of these methodologies, showing the importance of bringing together different categories of evidence to shed light on the textile industry in the late antique Mediterranean (Stauffer 2008). Dozens of surviving papyrus fragments depict a repertory of floral and vegetal motifs frequently seen in the period's textiles (Figure 19). The sheets might have been used to entice customers, but they may also have been used to transmit patterns among weavers, perhaps serving as aide-mémoire during the weaving process itself or as training guides for new weavers. The similarities of the motifs to other media also hint at possible crossover between workshops, likely located in close proximity to one another in the city or landscape.

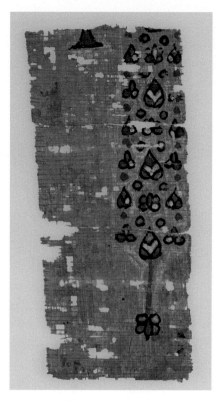

Figure 19 Model sheet, sixth-century papyrus. © Staatliche Museen zu Berlin – Ägyptisches Museum und Papyrussammlung, inv. nr. P 7766/a. Photo: M. Krutzsch.

The textiles themselves are also an important source of evidence for late antique and Byzantine textile industry. Fabrics often feature mixed-and-matched borders and central scenes, indicating that there were selections of customizable motifs for artists and patrons to choose from when ordering dress and furnishing fabrics. A sixth-century hanging at Dumbarton Oaks (Figure 20), for example, features a similar border and central scene to a more complete hanging of the same period now preserved at the Brooklyn Museum (Figure 21). The pieces' technical details are also alike, pointing perhaps to standardized workshop practice. When analyzed together, archaeological, material, and textual evidence like that discussed here can help clarify the role that weavers and patrons played in selecting and recombining different motifs as they ordered dress and furnishing textiles in innumerable workshops across Egypt.

Figure 20 Fragment of a hanging with two figures in arcades. Egypt, ca. sixth century. Dimensions: H. (warp) 42.0 cm × W. (weft) 63.2 cm (16 9/16 × 24 7/8 in.). Technique/material: Tapestry weave in polychrome wool. © Byzantine collection, Dumbarton Oaks Research Library and Collection, Washington, DC, BZ.1970.43.

Figure 21 Figures in niches or arcades, sixth–eighth century (probably). Medium: Wool. Dimensions: 102.9 × 147.3 cm (40 1/2 × 58 in.). Brooklyn Museum, Charles Edwin Wilbour Fund, 46.128a–b. Creative Commons-BY, photo: Brooklyn Museum.

The history of Byzantine silk production remains especially murky, despite the popular association of the material with the imperial court, thanks to depictions of sumptuous silks in the period's visual culture, as in the mosaics at San Vitale in Ravenna (see Figure 37). A rich terminology in textual sources is at times hard to square with the surviving objects, which are in turn challenging to date and attribute securely (Galliker 2015a; Galliker 2017). According to Procopius (act. sixth century), during the time of Emperor Justinian (r. 527–565) two Eastern Syriac monks smuggled silkworm eggs in their walking sticks from Central Asia into Byzantium, in a tale reminiscent of the Chinese Silk Princess mentioned in section 3.1 (Procopius trans. Dewing 1928, VIII, xvii: 226–229). Though the industry did thrive under Justinian's patronage, silk was in reality already being woven in the Eastern Mediterranean as early as the fourth century, before this story supposedly takes place. Silk production was closely guarded due to the high value of the goods produced and the sophistication of the weaving technology itself (Thomas 2012). The most luxurious Byzantine silks featured large repeating patterns of animals, mythological figures, hunting scenes, and floral and jeweled motifs in multiple colors, following visual and technological traditions seen in Central Asian (Sogdian) and Chinese silks. Perhaps the most famous of this so-called imperial group is a large-format silk depicting the explicitly Christian theme of the Annunciation (Figure 22). Today

Figure 22 Fragment of samite with scene of the *Annunciation,* five-color silk serge, Dimensions: 33.6 × 68.7 cm (roundels 32 × 33 cm). From the "treasury" of the Chapel of the *Sancta Sanctorum* in the Lateran Palace, Rome, Musei Vaticani, cat. 61231. Photograph © Governorate of the Vatican City State-Directorate of the Vatican Museums.

held in the Vatican, it is one of many Byzantine five-color silks held in European church treasuries, presumably arriving there as diplomatic gifts or through trade, as will be discussed Section 7.

High-status silk remained tightly controlled in Byzantium for many centuries, thanks to the close association of sericulture with imperial economic and diplomatic interests. The *Book of the Eparch*, a tenth-century source describing the regulation of guilds in Constantinople, for example, lists numerous categories of merchants and workshops owners involved in the silk industry, such as those selling silk garments, manufacturing purple silks, and selling imported "Syrian" silks, so-called because they were associated with production centers in those areas (Koder 1991). The text demonstrates how imperial silk factories and the sale of silk were tightly controlled by government officials with close ties to the empire's fiscal activities, such as coinage and minting. Byzantine lead seals are an important source of information for understanding these associations, because they name the individuals who played specialized roles in silk production and trade (Oikonomides 1986). The *kommerkiarios*, a government official charged with collecting taxes, was also involved in regulating silk production and trade.[4] These officials' seals sometimes even feature their names alongside images of the emperor, attesting to the high-level operations of the silk industry and its ties to the power of state. Similar associations of textiles with the imperial power of the fisc are seen in the Islamic world in precisely these same centuries. In Abbasid Baghdad, for example, the *dar al-tiraz* (imperial textile workshop) produced formulations and calligraphic conventions used on textiles and coins alike, and the officials charged with managing the workshop were also associated with the mint in its capacities to produce coinage and collect taxes (Stillman et al. 2012).

Though Constantinople has traditionally received the most attention in scholarship on the Byzantine silk production, recent work has raised questions about the ubiquity of the industry. Workshops producing high-quality, multicolor Byzantine silks were also located in the important Egyptian metropolis Alexandria, in Syria, and very likely in other parts of the Mediterranean. In the past, scholars attempted to link "groups" of silks to specific locations according to their perceived style and according to references in textual sources. Today, however, scholars hesitate to associate extant Byzantine textiles, like those in the "Lion Tamer" group, to precise places of production (see Figure 7). The evidence increasingly suggests that there were in fact numerous factories weaving silks that

---

[4] www.doaks.org/resources/seals/byzantine-seals#b_start=0&c21=Kommerkiarios.

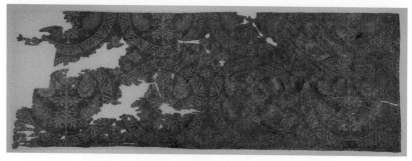

Figure 23 Fragment. Egypt? Syria? Seventh–ninth century. Dimensions: H. (warp) 34.0 cm × W. (weft) 97.0 cm (13 3/8 × 38 3/16 in.). Medium/ technique: Weft-faced compound twill (samite) in polychrome silk. © Byzantine Collection, Dumbarton Oaks Research Library and Collection, Washington, DC, BZ.1977.2.

Figure 24 Fragment of a silk clavus, sixth–ninth century. Dimensions: 37 cm (14 1/2 in) × 4.3 cm (1 5/8 in.). Abegg-Stiftung, CH-3132 Riggisberg, inv. nr. 2002 © Abegg-Stiftung, CH-3132 Riggisberg, 2003. Photo: Christoph von Viràg.

Figure 25 Textile fragment with hunting scene, eighth century, attributed to
Egypt or Syria. Medium: Silk; samite. Dimensions: H. 24.1 cm (9 1/2 in.) ×
W. 17.1 cm (6 3/4 in.). Metropolitan Museum of Art, New York, Rogers Fund,
1951, accession number: 51.57. Open access CC0.

underwent different levels of quality control, reflecting a more fluid
dynamic in the flow of technological knowhow and finished products
around the Mediterranean.

Large numbers of surviving two-color silks from Byzantine Egypt are perhaps the strongest evidence for this wider scale of production. These silks have
been associated with sites in Egypt, including Antinoë (Antinoöpolis) and
Akhmim (Panopolis), because of the large numbers of fragments excavated
there (El-Sayed and Fluck 2020). Silks of this kind feature medallions set in
repeating rows, often dominated by floral motifs or hunting figures. Their
limited color range and smaller repeat units set them apart from five-color
imperial silks with monumental patterns, indicating that the former textiles were
produced on less technologically sophisticated drawlooms. Silk fabric of this kind

was produced in bolts, as evidenced in a rare example of salmon-pink and beige silk at Dumbarton Oaks that preserves the larger repeating pattern in rows (Figure 23). The pieces were then cut from these larger formats into shapes for tunic decorations, meaning that a very small amount of precious silk could be efficiently and cost-effectively used to maximum effect on numerous garments (Figure 24). Surviving evidence suggests that the production of these more modest, but still luxurious two-colored silks lasted over several centuries in Egypt into the early Islamic period, indicating continuity of this luxury craft industry despite widespread cultural change. A group of this kind of silk featuring riding Amazons, for example, can be confidently dated to the first centuries of Islam, thanks to the mirrored Arabic inscription reading *"bismillah"* ("In the Name of God") above the riders' heads (Figure 25).

3.3 Mobility and Transmission

The stories of how silk-making technologies were transmitted makes clear that these were based in human knowledge. In other words, it was not enough to know that silk came from worms which were fed with mulberry leaves. The sericulturist had to have specific knowledge of the various steps that turned silkworm eggs and mulberry seeds into the finished product of spun silk.[5] So too the weavers of fine textiles, with their knowledge of how to set up a loom and weave specific patterns, also represented repositories of technological knowledge (Burns 2014). In Asia throughout the period under consideration, weavers trained in one geograph-ical region were often relocated to another either by force or for economic reasons, bringing their technical proficiencies with them. Indeed, the Chinese and Central Asian historical record between 300 and 1400 preserves many instances of weavers and artisans being relocated over vast geographic dis-tances, bringing specific types of weaving knowledge with them.

The spread of certain motifs such as the pearl roundel (Figure 26), which became ubiquitous across Eurasia during the sixth through eleventh centuries, points as much to the movement of objects with designs that were imitated across media as it does to weavers and textile designers who favored certain patterns and weave structures (Canepa 2014). The names given to certain textiles also point to the origins (or imagined origins) of certain weave struc-tures. For example, the Arabic word *zaytuni*, used in an eleventh-century document found in Cairo Geniza, is thought to be at the origin of the word "satin" (for the Cairo Geniza, see discussion Section 5.3). *Zaytuni* may refer to the Chinese port city of Quanzhou, called Çaiton/Zaitun/Zayton in non-Chinese

---

[5] www.youtube.com/watch?v=77ktNSPFbwQ&ab_channel=Vox.

Figure 26 Child's coat with ducks in pearl medallions, 700s, probably Sogdia (present-day Uzbekistan), China, Tang dynasty. Medium/technique: Silk, weft-faced compound twill weave (samite). Dimensions: Width across shoulders 84.5 cm (33 1/4 in.); length back of neck to hem 51.4 cm (20 1/4 in.). Cleveland Museum of Art, Cleveland, Purchase from the J. H. Wade Fund, 1996.2.1. Open access CC0.

sources in the thirteenth and fourteenth centuries, which was arguably the point of export for the first satin weaves to the West (Shea 2018; Shea 2021a). Indeed, many cloths and weaves had a geographical association.

This was also the case within China. Traditionally, China is divided by the Yangtze River into north and south. North of the Yangtze is associated with compound weaves, especially *jin* – a Chinese word that can refer to a variety of compound, polychrome, and patterned weaves, including samite, taqueté, and certain types of brocades. Weaves like damask and gauze are associated with the south, the Jiangnan ("south of the Yangtze River") region. Beginning in the Tang dynasty, gold-woven textiles (lampas, brocades) were associated with the "north," which in this period expanded to include present-day Mongolia, the steppe, and Central Asia). While this geographical distinction is a generalization, it is an association that goes back hundreds of years — historical texts assign production of certain types of cloth to the north or south.

However, the reality is more complex, in part due to the displacement of textile workers who would weave textile types associated with one region in their new homes. Displacement of artisans, especially weavers, occurred consistently in East Asia between 300 and 1400 and happened on a particularly large scale during the Mongol period. For example, as noted in the *History of the Yuan Dynasty* (*Yuan shi*), at the beginning of the Mongol period in China (the 1220s), 300 households of weavers from Central Asia, trained in weaving with gold thread, were relocated to Hongzhou, a court-weaving center near the capital (present-day Beijing). There they worked alongside 300 households of captured Chinese and Central Asian weavers specialized in weaving and coarse woolen cloth-making. These captured weavers had been working for the Jin dynasty, conquered by the Mongols in 1215, in their last capital of Bianjing (Shea 2020; Song [1370] 1976; Wardwell and Watt 1988).

In the Mediterranean context, Jane Burns remarks that specific weaves made by displaced textile workers sometimes went by the weaver's place of origin, even after they were moved to a new location (Burns 2014). In addition, as David Jacoby has pointed out, while the practice of naming specific weaves after geographic locations was widespread by writers in the Muslim world, the place-name designation often endured long after the weave was made in a variety of locations – as was the case with satin, which, while originating in southern China, was also eventually woven in West Asia and the Mediterranean (Jacoby 2004).

It is, however, important to note that inscriptions on textiles noting the place of manufacture were not always genuine. A textile now in the Boston Museum of Fine Art, for instance, carries an inscription with the claim that it was made in Baghdad (Figure 27). Thought to have come from the tomb of bishop Pedro de Osma (d. 1109) in the cathedral of Burgo de Osma (Spain), it has become clear based on analysis of the weaving technique that the textile was produced under Almoravid rule in North Africa or Spain (Elsberg and Guest 1934; Mühlemann

Figure 27 Fragment with wrestling lions and harpies, Spanish (probably Almería), Almoravid, early twelfth century. Medium/technique: Silk lampas with supplementary discontinuous metal-wrapped patterning wefts. Dimensions: 50 × 43 cm (19 11/16 × 16 15/16 in.). Museum of Fine Arts, Boston, Ellen Page Hall Fund, accession number 33.371. Photograph © 2023 Museum of Fine Arts, Boston.

2022; Partearroyo 1992; Shepherd 1957). Whether to call this a fake, assuming malicious and deceitful intent on the part of the maker, or to regard it as a more innocent playing up of an important, prestigious brand (that is, Baghdad as the capital of the Abbasid caliphate and a major cultural center of the medieval Islamic world) is up for debate. Clearly, producers and merchants manipulated textiles in order to achieve higher gains: in the Islamic world, textiles were included in so-called *hisba* manuals describing the rules of the market (Ghabin 2009: 216–245). These rules were enforced by the market overseer (*muhtasib* in Arabic) who was responsible for keeping dishonest practices in check that could range from false attribution to places of production to the use of inferior dyes.

We must also consider that, even though Baghdad was probably the most important center of textile production in the Eastern Islamic world up until the Mongol conquest of the city in 1258, we have very few textiles in hand that are clearly attributed to this place of production (Otavsky 1997). Textile production in al-Andalus, the parts of present-day Spain and Portugal that were under Muslim rule from the eighth to the fifteenth centuries (with shifting territories), is documented as early as the tenth century when royal workshops existed in Cordoba (Dodds 1992: 224–225). While only a few fragments, mostly in tapestry weave, survive from the early period, evidence of a much larger production exists especially for the eleventh and twelfth centuries, when cities such as Almería and Malaga were major centers of textile production (Partearroyo 1992). Famously, the Muslim geographer al-Idrisi (d. 1165) described the many types of luxury textiles produced in Almería, and emphasized the great number of looms that were active in the city (English translation in Blessing 2019). Figured silks were among the most luxurious fabrics produced here. These textiles were prized not only in al-Andalus but also in Christian-ruled areas of the Iberian Peninsula and in France (Feliciano 2005; Kinoshita 2004).

4 Trade

Trade and industry are intimately connected, as it was through the movement of people and objects that different types of textiles came to be produced across Eurasia. The stories about how the technology for making silk came to be smuggled out of China into the Tarim Basin in the headdress of a princess, and from China into Byzantium, in the staffs of Eastern Syriac monks, are famous examples of (clandestine) technological transfer facilitated by diplomatic trade. Records of displaced silk weavers exemplify the spread of human knowledge often resulting from war or other violence. The period of 300–1400 was a time of connectivity across Eurasia, with the overland and, later, maritime, routes connecting Asia between Chang'an (modern day Xi'an) and Constantinople and arguably extending east as far as Japan and west to present-day Sweden (Hu 2017; Walker 2010). In the Mediterranean zone other routes connected North Africa to Spain and France (Burns 2014). As many scholars have pointed out, the Silk Roads was not a unified highway but a network of more local trade routes. Few objects made the journey from the Byzantine Empire to China before the sixth century, but as the centuries wore on, various groups, including the Byzantines, Genoese, Abbasids, Mamluks, Sogdians, Chinese, and Mongols, among others, exchanged quantities of material such as ceramics, metalware, spices, and most importantly for this Element, textiles.

Textiles functioned in a few different ways as a trading commodity. On a basic level, unpatterned plain-weave silk, or self-patterned compound silk, were used as currency in various locations, including the Tarim Basin (present-day Xinjiang Province, China), and during the Fatimid period in Alexandria, Egypt (Ansari 2013; Burns 2014; Goitein 1967, 1973; Hansen 2016). In imperial China, households had to give a certain amount of the cloth that they produced to the government as a tax (Kuhn and Zhao 2012). Woven silks were bought, sold, and gifted at various levels of society. Secular and ecclesiastical courts exchanged highly complex luxury fabrics, especially silks and silks woven or embroidered with metallic threads, as an integral part of diplomatic relations. Trade and gift exchange also encouraged the spread of motifs, such as the pearl roundel, found as a decorative motif on textiles woven and used from Egypt to Japan during the period from 500–1000 (see Figure 26).

In late Roman, Byzantine, and early Islamic Egypt, archaeological and textual evidence attests to a rich trade in finished cloth imported from outside the region and movement of people bringing finished textiles with them (Thomas 2017). The cemeteries of Antinoë, for example, preserve a wide array of silks and tapestry-woven dress and furnishing fabrics whose design motifs and technical characteristics can be associated with Sasanian Persian traditions (Calament and Durand 2013). Some of the textiles were brought there by military officers during a period of Sasanian occupation in the seventh century. For example, two extraordinary fifth- to seventh-century Persian-style riding coats found there typify the kind of dress associated with governmental authorities (Figure 28). And motifs on Sasanian silks found in Antinoë, for example, appear also on contemporary tapestry-woven fabrics (Figure 29) whose technical characteristics suggest Egyptian production (Bénazeth and Dal-Prà 1995). In this way we can see that the arrival of high-quality textiles from abroad could spur demand for imitations among local consumers drawn to the prestige of the imported textiles' motifs, colors, or designs (Dospěl Williams 2019).

Figure 28 Riding coat, 440–640 (radiocarbon date, 95 percent probability).
Medium/technique: Plain weave in blue-green sheep's wool and cashmere;
applied borders in tablet weave of polychrome wool and undyed linen; patches
of fabric in plain weave of undyed linen to reinforce armpits and hemline.
Dimensions: 120 cm. (47 1/4 in) × 252 cm (8 ft. 3 1/4 in). Inv. 9695
© Staatliche Museen zu Berlin, Skulpturensammlung und Museum für
Byzantinische Kunst, photo: Antje Voigt.

The Red Sea was also a major trade route for textiles from the late antique through Islamic period, especially cotton. Excavations at the Roman ports at Berenike and Quseir al-Qadim in Egypt, for example, revealed fragments of cotton textiles, though there is some debate as to whether these represent locally Egyptian-made fabrics or imported Indian ones (Kelley 2019; Wild and Wild 2014). Egyptian-grown cotton – attested in numerous documentary texts about agricultural production – was presumably exported as raw material through the Red Sea and beyond, while finished Indian cloth was in turn transported into Egypt along maritime routes. Ruth Barnes' trail-blazing work, for example, has focused on "Indo-Egyptian" textiles – examples found in Egypt with stylistic qualities linking them to Gujarat (see Figure 14). Radiocarbon dates for these textiles ranged from roughly the eleventh through seventeenth centuries, attesting to the long duration of trade from the Fatimid through Mamluk (and later) eras (Barnes 1997). That archaeological finds include a mix of Indian-made fabrics of this style and Egyptian ones again attests to the creative role of trade in spurring local production and imitation.

Trade in textiles occurred across the overland Silk Roads consistently between 300 and 1400, with peaks occurring during the Chinese Tang dynasty and the Mongol period. Although much of it was restricted to local use, objects, including textiles, occasionally traveled from the Mediterranean region to China or the reverse. The Tang dynasty saw a fashion for Central Asian-style clothing and textile patterns, for both men and women, in the capital of Chang'an (Chen 2019).

Figure 29 Fragment of a hanging with horses and lions. Eastern Mediterranean,
ca. sixth or seventh century. Dimensions: H. (warp) 166.5 cm × W. (weft)
80.0 cm (65 9/16 × 31 1/2 in.). Tapestry weave in polychrome wool and undyed
linen. © Byzantine Collection, Dumbarton Oaks Research Library and
Collection, Washington, DC, BZ.1939.13.

Arab and Persian merchant communities were established in the port city of
Quanzhou in the ninth century and continued to flourish during the Song dynasty
(Clark 1995; Lo 2012; Ptak 1998). Material remains of this trade are found in
ceramics rather than textiles, with a few exceptions.

During the Mongol period exchange across Eurasia occurred on a grander scale
than in previous centuries. Distances covered by individual travelers increased, and
following in the footsteps of Franciscan missionaries, merchants and diplomatic
envoys began to make the trip from the Mediterranean to China (Jackson 2017). The
most famous of these was the Venetian merchant Marco Polo, whose published

account of his travels to China via Central Asia, the *Description of the World* (*Devisement du monde*, 1298), devotes a considerable amount of space to descriptions of different types of textiles he encountered during his trip (Polo trans. Pelliot and Moule 1976; Polo trans. Latham 1958). Marco Polo's voyage took him overland through Central Asia to China via the well-established trade routes of the Silk Road. On his way back, he sailed along the equally well-established maritime routes that connected southern China to the Indian Ocean and Arabian seas. Back in the Mediterranean, too, woven textiles from Byzantine and Islamic lands were traded through major ports especially in Greece, Cyprus, Italy, and Spain. Local sericulture also developed in these areas and resulted in major industries in their own right (Jacoby 1991–92, 2008, 2016, 2017). For example, in the second half of the thirteenth century, thanks to a strong network of Genoese and Venetian merchants, gold-woven "Tartar" textiles (*panni tartarici*) (Figure 30) were increasingly available in northern Italian cities, which in turn impacted the Genoese, Lucchese, and Venetian silk industries (Jacoby 2004; Monnas 2010; Wardwell 1988–89). Coming for the most part from the Mongol-ruled Ilkhanate, but also from Mamluk territories, such silks introduced designs that integrated motifs from China, Central Asia, and the Islamic world which were imitated in Italian silks, including the phoenix, lotus, pinecone/pomegranate, fungus-shaped clouds, crescent moons, vegetal and floral scrolls, and geometric patterns. The significance of these patterns likely changed as motifs were conveyed from East Asia to Central and West Asia and again into the Mediterranean, shedding certain cultural associations while gaining others. The phoenix, for example,

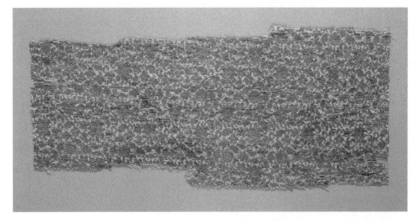

Figure 30 Textile with floral pattern. Late thirteenth–mid-fourteenth century. Central Asia. Medium: Silk and metallic thread lampas. Dimensions: 12.1 × 27.9 cm (4 3/4 × 11 in.). Metropolitan Museum of Art, New York, Rogers Fund, 1919, accession number: 19.191.3. Open access CC0.

a mythological bird which symbolized the empress in China, sometimes appears in the guise of the mythological *simurgh* in the Persian context, but as a phoenix once more, with Christological significance, in the Italian context (Monnas 2010; Walker 2010; Wardwell 1988–89). Silks from the Mongol Empire and Islamic world also introduced new weave structures to weaving centers such as Genoa, Lucca, and Venice, including taffeta, satin, velvet, and a variety of lampas weaves — these weaves were particularly suited to imitating eastern silks (Monnas 2010). These Italian centers of silk production were also important trade centers with contacts to the Islamic world, especially the Ottomans. Trade with fabrics went back and forth between Italy and the Ottoman Empire, where Bursa emerged as a center of textile production in the late fifteenth century (Çizakça 1980; Phillips 2021: 49–53). Mutual influence through trade with brocaded velvets, in particular, led to similarities in production in the Italian and Ottoman centers, to the extent that some sixteenth-century textiles can only be securely attributed through technical analysis of weave structure and dyes, rather than by stylistic means (Contadini 2013).

5 Dress

It is difficult to make general observations about dress across Eurasia during the medieval period, not only because of the breadth of different cultures but also because the surviving material, visual, archaeological, and textual evidence is incomplete and sometimes contradictory. Still, there were some commonalities. For instance, court dress in many places, including China, the Islamic empires and polities, and the Byzantine Empire, was highly regulated.[6] In cultural hubs as capital cities or courts, sumptuary regulations were enacted, to a greater or lesser extent, on official and nonelite populations. Such laws generally stipulated the types of fabric and tailoring allowed to different classes of people, but also included restrictions on decorative elements, such as specific designs and costly materials such as gold thread. In many places, these regulations seem to have been specifically aimed at women's dress (Dospěl Williams 2018a). The ways in which governments attempted to restrain people from wearing specific clothing is a useful way of understanding what people of that time were wearing. Many places in medieval Eurasia had rules about dress, and the norms for what was worn at court differed from what the general population wore, although more evidence exists, in terms of surviving textiles, pictorial evidence, and texts for courtly dress than for the quotidian dress of regular people. In this section we will investigate evidence for both courtly dress and

---

[6] https://byzantiumandfriends.podbean.com/e/62-byzantine-dress-and-fashion-with-jennifer-ball-and-elizabeth-dospel-williams/.

dress outside of the court. People did not necessarily follow the rules of a central authority in their dress (defying regulations seems to be a universal human impulse).

5.1 Regional and Historical Changes to Dress

What we consider to be within the political borders of the People's Republic of China today actually represents a great diversity of groups and peoples, all with their own dressing norms and often with very different textile making traditions. While Chinese historians have kept meticulous records for at least the last 2,500 years which gives the illusion of continuity of culture, the geographic expanse over which these texts had an impact fluctuated over time. Stipulations for what people were supposed to wear according to rank and status in China existed from before the Han dynasty, and are articulated, for example, in the *Book of Rites*, a Confucian text which was compiled during the late Warring States period, ca. 475–221 BCE (Legge 1967). Strict norms for dress that included the types of fabrics, colors, and decorative elements continued to be articulated by the central authority until the end of imperial rule in China in 1911 and are recorded in dynastic histories and other official texts. However, the rigid norms articulated in historical texts are not a complete reflection of what people actually wore during different moments in history.

The implementation of sumptuary regulations also coincides with greater choice of dress for both elites and nonelites. In China, for example, the Tang dynasty (ca. 618–907) during the height of Silk Road trade, was a period where both members of the court and the general population of the capital city of Chang'an wore an increasingly dazzling array of patterned silks, inspired by Central Asian textiles and dress. This resulted in the court passing restrictions in the types of dress and textiles allowed to the general population alongside poetic admonitions aimed at elite women by court officials.

Faced with differences beween the regulations of the Han dynasty on the one hand, and excavations in present-day Xinjiang Province, on the other hand, we must recognize two things: first, that there was a diversity of dress beyond what is recorded in official records, and second, the fact that rules applied to officials in the court in the capital city of Chang'an does not grant us a complete understanding of "Han" textiles found in sites where the Han army was present, but local cultures, rather than Han norms, may have been more impactful.

The diversity of dress for which there is evidence and the contrast between courtly norms and what elites were wearing continued during the millennium of our focus. How, then, to determine what people were wearing across Eurasia between 300 and 1400? As in earlier periods, official texts give us some information about courtly etiquette and societal norms. Equally important for a more holistic understanding of a given period, however, are material sources such as excavated or otherwise preserved period textiles, pictorial depictions of dress, sculptural representations of dress, and texts such as inventories, travel accounts, or poetry. We will begin with an examination of court dress and the relevance of hierarchical robing systems during this period before moving onto the broader array of dress available to elites (and others) during this period.

5.2 Court Dress

Evidence for court dress during the period covered here is generally more robust than for other types of dress. This is due to the preservation of historical records written for or about different courts such as legal documents that stipulated dress codes, descriptions of various courtly ceremonies, and inventories. Additionally, a greater number of textiles corresponding to court dress, or at least the dress of elites, has survived than for the dress of other people in the form of grave goods and preserved in the treasuries of temples and churches, especially in East Asia and Europe. Pictorial evidence for court dress in the form of illustrated manuscripts, court-commissioned paintings, religious paintings featuring donor figures, and funerary art also provide important context for courtly dress across Eurasia. While these sources are also valuable for evidence of dress outside of a courtly setting, they often focus on the court or on elite subjects. Similarly, representations of textiles used within space — such as carpets and curtains — often appear in images of palatial contexts.

5.2.1 Court Dress in Inner and East Asia

As mentioned Section 5.1, official regulations concerning dress in China have existed for at least 2,500 years. This is important to note because courtly rituals and their accompanying dress were built on precedent. In other words, during the period of 300–1400 in China, courts looked to what they understood to be historical practice as grounding for their rituals. Thus, the types of dress worn by the emperor, the empress, princes, and officials for court ceremonies was, at least on paper, conservative and slow to change. Different types of dress were prescribed for specific rituals, and the emperor and empress wore a variety of different more or less elaborate clothes and headwear for specific occasions. In addition, court officials were organized into highly regulated ranks, which was expressed sartorially by the color and shade of their dress. In addition, "Chinese" court dress, and in particular Tang dynasty court dress, impacted the court dress of courts outside of China. These included the court dress of groups originating in present-day Mongolia such as the Xianbei (fl. first–seventh centuries), Khitans (fl. ninth–twelfth centuries), and Jurchens (fl. twelfth–thirteenth centuries); kingdoms on the Korean peninsula during the Three Kingdoms period (ca. first century BCE–seventh century CE), Unified Silla (ca. 676–935); and the courts of Asuka (ca. 538–710), Nara (ca. 710–794), and Heian (ca. 794–1185) period Japan.

One example of Chinese imperial court dress is the emperor's *mian* crown and dragon-patterned robe which was worn during sacrificial ceremonies. The *mian* was a type of flat crown, like a mortarboard, with jade pendants hanging from the front and back (Figure 31). Pictorial evidence of the *mian* crown and accompanying robe adorned with auspicious symbols (including the moon, sun, and dragons) exists from the Tang dynasty, but the description of the emperor's sacrificial wear in the *Book of Rites*, "The son of Heaven, when sacrificing, wore [the cap] with the twelve long pendants of beads of jade hanging down from its top before and behind, and the robe embroidered with dragons," could easily correspond to what was later called the *mian* crown and a variation of the robe with auspicious symbols (Legge 1967). The dragon was associated with the emperor and the phoenix with the empress from an early period, although they were not restricted to imperial use until the Yuan dynasty in a ruling of 1297, with more specifics about the type of dragon outlined in an edict of 1314 (Chen et al. 2011; Huang 1986; Song 1976[1370]).

The dress of court officials in China was, until the Mongol-ruled Yuan dynasty, organized by color, which changed with the seasons. There were nine official ranks, with ninth being the lowest and first the highest. Regulations pertaining to an official extended to his household; women's clothing and adornments were thus regulated by their husband or father's rank. In the Yuan dynasty the nine ranks of the Chinese bureaucracy were maintained, but officials were restricted in the materials they were permitted to use rather than by color. Bureaucratic distinction by color is illustrated in the robes worn by civil and

Figure 31 The thirteen emperors, 歷代帝王圖 卷 (傳閻 立本) attributed to Yan Liben (Chinese, about 600–673), Tang dynasty, second half of the seventh century. Medium/technique: Ink and color on silk. Dimensions: 51.3 × 531 cm (20 3/16 × 209 1/16 in.). Museum of Fine Arts, Boston, Waldo Ross Collection, accession number 31.643. Photograph © 2023 Museum of Fine Arts, Boston.

military officials of the Northern Song court on parade in the eleventh-century painting, *Illustration of the Imperial Guard of Honor* (*Dajia lubu tu* 大駕鹵簿 圖).[7] These official robes would have been made of silk and were generally monochrome. In the Yuan dynasty, officials of the highest rank (ranks one and two) were permitted to wear robes with all over use of gold, probably something approximating *nasij* (something like the fabric in Figure 12) or similar to the caftan in the David Collection (Figure 36), while those of the third rank were permitted repeat patterns in gold such as tabby weave silks with brocaded repeat pattern in gold thread (Figure 32) (Shea 2020). Courts in Japan and the Korean peninsula in the sixth through ninth centuries had their own rank systems, more or less adapted from the Tang Chinese system. As in China, in the courts of Japan and the Korean peninsula, official rank was tied to particular colors and shades of dress which changed with the seasons (von Verschuer 2008).

In Heian Japan, elite men wore three principal categories of dress, ceremonial dress, court dress, and informal dress, while elite women wore formal, semi-formal, and informal dress, depending on the occasion. Costume type and hue

Figure 32 Brocade with lotus flowers, Northern China, Yuan dynasty, 1200s– mid-1300s. Medium: Silk; tabby, brocaded; gold thread. Dimensions: Overall – 58.4 × 67 cm (23 × 26 3/8 in.); mounted: 68.6 × 77.5 cm (27 × 30 1/2 in.). The Cleveland Museum of Art, John L. Severance Fund 1994.293. Open access CC0.

---

[7] https://en.wikipedia.org/wiki/File:Da_jia_lu_bu_tu_shu_flag_6_(51178031839).jpg.

was highly regulated for both men and women. Although the form of Heian dress differed from Tang Chinese dress, the relationship between color and rank were rooted in continental practice (Dusenbury 2015). The main visual source for Heian court dress is the illustrated scroll of the *Tale of Genji* (*Genji monogatari emaki*) from the early twelfth century.[8] In various scenes of the scroll, we find examples of men's court dress, or *sokutai* (belted costume) and women's formal dress, in particular the court lady's multilayered robes, the *nyōbo shozoku* (court lady's costume), later nicknamed *juni hitoe* (twelve robes). Court ladies' costume involved the layering of twelve separate kimono-style robes, made of monochrome, plain-weave silk, with gradually shorter hems and sleeves to show the layers underneath (Dusenbury 2015; von Verschuer 2008).

As the borrowing of aspects of Chinese ritual and dress by courts in Japan and the Korean peninsula indicate, Chinese court dress was recognized as a dress of political power in the East Asian sphere, especially during the Tang dynasty. Indeed, the Tang's cosmopolitan capital of Chang'an at the eastern end of the overland Silk Roads was perhaps the most impactful cultural center in East Asia in the seventh, eighth, and ninth centuries. Even after the fall of the Tang, its impact continued to reverberate in aspects of dress at the Heian court in Japan, the Goreyo (918–1392) and Joseon (ca. 1392–1897) courts on the Korean peninsula, and the Liao (ca. 907–1125), Jin (ca. 1115–1234), and Song (ca. 960–1279) courts in China.

The adoption of types of Tang and Song court dress by non-Chinese groups such as the Khitan, who ruled as the Liao dynasty, and the Jurchen, who conquered Liao territory and some Song territory and ruled as the Jin dynasty, indicates the continued importance of Chinese court dress in East Asia. These two "nonnative" Chinese dynasties ruled simultaneously to the Song dynasty, whose territory was restricted to southern parts of China. In the context of the Liao and the Jin Chinese court dress was referred to as "Han-style dress" which was to be worn during Chinese-style ceremonies such as sacrificing to the ancestors. This was distinct from their own types of court dress, called "state-style dress" in the *History of the Liao Dynasty* (*Liao shi*) (Shea 2020). State-style dress included clothing that was worn during important events such as hunts and other banquets and likely was made of silk woven with gold, such as in the famed "swan hunt" textile from the Jin dynasty (Figure 33). Married women in the Liao and Jin dynasties wore clothing and fabrics appropriate to the rank of their husbands, while unmarried women dressed according to their father's rank. Liao women living in the northern part of the empire consistently wore "state-style" dress, while those living in the

---

[8] https://en.wikipedia.org/wiki/Genji_Monogatari_Emaki. Unfortunately, we were unable to clear image rights to include images from the *Tale of Genji*.

southern part of the empire dressed in "Han" style, closer in type to Tang, and later, Song dress. In the Jin dynasty, Song-style dress was adopted by women more broadly, although neither the Liao nor the Jin practiced foot-binding, which began in southern China during the Song dynasty (Shea 2020; Wang 2000). The use of gold threads in elite clothing of the Liao and Jin dynasties is a characteristic that distinguishes them from elite dress of the Song dynasty, and the use of gold thread in complex weaves became more elaborate and widespread in court dress during the Mongol-ruled Yuan dynasty (ca. 1260–1368). The Mongol period ushered in some significant changes to the court dress system.

During the Yuan dynasty, the Mongols created a new sartorial idiom that both adopted their preimperial dress to a courtly context and borrowed from earlier groups such as the Khitan (Liao dynasty) and Jurchen (Jin dynasty). The emphasis during this period was, however, on Mongol, not Chinese, identity, and the Mongols did not follow a dual court dress system as had been the case under the Liao and Jin (Shea 2020). The dynastic history of the Yuan, the *History of the Yuan Dynasty* (*Yuan shi*), compiled after the fall of the Yuan dynasty,

Figure 33 Textile with swan hunt, Jin dynasty (1115–1234), twelfth–thirteenth century, China. Medium: Plain-weave silk brocaded with gold leaf-wrapped leather strips. Dimensions: 58.5 × 62.2 cm (23 × 24 1/2 in.). Metropolitan Museum of Art, New York, Purchase, Ann Eden Woodward Foundation Gift and Rogers Fund, 1989, accession number: 1989.282. Open access CC0.

includes the familiar, Chinese-style description of the emperor's dress and the dress of his officials. It is possible that the Yuan emperors partook in certain Chinese-style ceremonies in a show of appropriation of these rituals. However, the dress of power during Mongol rule was not Chinese court dress, but Mongol court dress, which is also described in detail in the *History of the Yuan Dynasty*.

The Mongols had confederated two generations before the founding of the Yuan dynasty by Khubilai Khan (r. 1260–1294) under Khubilai's grandfather, Chinggis Khan (r. 1206–1227). When Khubilai founded the Yuan dynasty in 1260, his court co-opted certain aspects of Liao, Song, and Jin dynasty ceremony and dress and combined these with Mongol-style clothing, namely a belted riding coat worn with trousers and boots, and rituals, such as mass gifting of clothing from the khan to his officials. Women, too, wore Mongol-style dress at court, which included an ample, wide-sleeved robe that tapered at the wrists and a tall headdress called a *boqta* (Figure 34 and Figure 35). In addition, the definitive elite textile of the Yuan dynasty, and Mongol Empire more broadly, was *nasij*, which usually referred to a gold-woven silk lampas. Gold-woven lampas was used for clothing and hats, as hanging panels to adorn the interior of the tents of Mongol rulers, and as sutra covers, among other materials (Shea 2021b). Examples of both men's

Figure 34 Covering for a *boqta* (*gugu guan*) headdress, silk and metallic thread lampas (*nasij*). China or Central Asia, Mongol period (thirteenth–mid-fourteenth century). China National Silk Museum, accession number 2722.

Figure 35 Anige (1245–1306), portrait of Chabi. Album leaf, ink, and colors on silk. Dimensions: Height: 61.5 cm, width 48 cm. National Palace Museum, Taipei. Open access.

Figure 36 Caftan sewn from a lampas-woven textile, silk with gilded lamella of animal substrate. Eastern Islamic world or China. First half of fourteenth century. Dimensions: H. incl. collar 139 cm; H. (shoulder to hem) 130 cm; W. incl. both sleeves 195 cm. The David Collection, Copenhagen, 23/2004, photograph: Pernille Klemp.

and women's court dress in lampas weaves have been excavated (Figure 36) (Shea 2018). The mass gifting of robes by the ruler to those who have sworn him allegiance during the Mongol period is connected to similar practices in Central Asia, which had existed for hundreds of years prior to Mongol conquest.

5.2.2 Court Dress in Byzantium

As in East and Central Asia, imperial dress in Byzantium was closely tied to court ceremonial (Ball 2005; Piltz 2013). The imperial garment, the *loros*, was emblematic of imperial power, changing relatively little over the centuries. Made of silk and covered in gemstones and pearls, the garment appears as early as the sixth century in Byzantine visual and textual sources, most notably on coins and ivories. The loros' sheer weight and opulence made it impractical for everyday dress, and it was thus presumably worn only for special formal ceremonies, such as investitures, diplomatic receptions, or religious rites, where the presence of the imperial office was meant to convey timeless authority and the emperor's unique role between church and state. The *loros* was in fact worn by both emperor and empress, with little gendered distinction in dress, in large part because its symbolic valences were more important than its association with any individual ruler.

If the *loros* could be seen as the relatively unchanging symbol of authority at the highest level of imperial ceremonial, other garments came to be associated with the court in other contexts. Gem- and pearl-studded gold crowns, special silken togas known as the *chlamys*, and red silken shoes were all part of the sartorial trappings of imperial power (Figure 37). Silk garments dyed in purple derived from murex shells, for example, were reserved for the garments of only the highest-ranking members of the emperor's family.[9] Purple silks were highly coveted beyond the Byzantine court: bishop Liutprand of Cremona (d. 972), ambassador of Holy Roman Emperor Otto I (d. 973) to Constantinople, was caught trying to smuggle such silks out on his way home in 968. As Liutprand describes with some outrage,[10] the wares were confiscated on the spot (Bauer and Rau 1971: 572–579; Bücheler 2019: 21–22; Mayr-Harting 2001). Because of such export restrictions, true purple textiles have rarely survived in Western treasuries (or elsewhere); one rare eleventh-century example with griffins in roundels (Figure 38) is held in the treasury of Valère Basilica in Sion, Switzerland (Fehlmann et al. 2019: 132–133).

By the late Byzantine period, further changes in imperial dress reflected changing social dynamics in Byzantine society and connections to neighboring cultures. Pisanello's drawings of the Byzantine emperor, John VIII Palaiologos

---

[9] https://archive.aramcoworld.com/issue/200604/millennia.of.murex.htm.
[10] https://sourcebooks.fordham.edu/source/liudprand1.asp.

Figure 37 Theodora and retinue, San Vitale, 547, Ravenna, Italy. Photograph by Patricia Blessing, 2015. Reproduced by permission of Opera di Religione della Diocesi di Ravenna.

Figure 38 Fragment of a dalmatica with griffins, Byzantium? Eleventh century. Silk dyed with purple. Dimensions: 51.3 × 107.50 cm. MV 12879, Dépôt du Chapitre cathédral de Sion © Musées cantonaux du Valais, Sion, Switzerland. Michel Martinez & Bernard Dubuis.

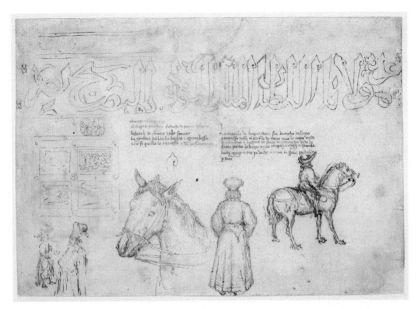

Figure 39 Antonio Pisanello, pen and dark brown ink on paper, 1438–39.
Musée du Louvre, Département des Arts Graphiques, MI 1062, recto.
© RNM-Grand Palais/ Art Resource NY/ Art Resource.

(r. 1425–48), for example, completed during the Council of Florence-Ferrara in ca. 1437–39, depict the ruler wearing a distinctive, tall hat with a pointy visor and *tiraz* prominently featuring Arabic script (Figure 39). Unusual hats had by this point become a fashionable statement among nonimperial Byzantine elites, while the fashion for wearing *tiraz* as part of elite dress derived from cross-Mediterranean encounters with these textiles as diplomatic gifts and trade goods.

Visual representations depicting Byzantine imperial dress in manuscripts, wall paintings, mosaics, ivories, coins, and other media attest to changes in the *loros* over time, yet no extant garments to corroborate these depictions. The survival of dress items associated with courts in Palermo, Sicily, however, offers some hint at the splendor of what was once worn in Byzantine imperial settings. A pair of thirteenth-century gloves, for example, is made of deep red silk finely embroidered with metallic thread and covered with hundreds of small pearls and luxurious enamel plaques (Figure 40). A splendid mantle featuring the name of the Norman king Roger II (1095–1154) in Arabic and the date 1133–34 features similarly ornate embroidery as well as gems, pearls, and enamel plaques (Figure 41). These examples demonstrate that in Byzantium and its cultural sphere, imperial dress was intended to dazzle viewers with splendor and to evoke the ruler's might through the use of rare materials and technologically advanced weavings and metalworking (Hoffman 2001).

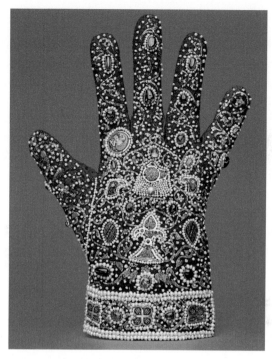

Figure 40 Gloves with enamels, Sicily, thirteenth century ? Kaiserliche Schatzkammer, Kunsthistorisches Museum Vienna, inv. WS XIII 11, 2013/8033. Image: KHM-Museumsverband.

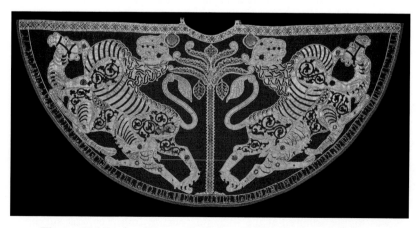

Figure 41 Mantle of Roger II, Sicily, twelfth century, Kaiserliche Schatzkammer, Kunsthistorisches Museum Vienna, inv. XIII 14. Image: KHM-Museumsverband.

The mantle of Roger II is also remarkable because it includes elements of Islamic court dress, especially with the presence of Arabic inscriptions that state the date of its making, and the place of production, the court workshops of Palermo (Tronzo 2001). Such dated inscriptions stating that a specific textile was made in a royal textile workshop (*dar al-tiraz* in Arabic) appeared on fabrics that were produced in court workshops in the Islamic world. Such textiles were never sold at market, but could be given as diplomatic gifts, or as signs of appreciation from the ruler to court officials. This practice of rulers giving robes of honor (*khilat* in Arabic) to notables and officials goes back to at least the eighth century as documented in textual sources, even though surviving examples are rare, and of later dates (Hambly 2001). This practice was closely connected to the development of *tiraz*, that is, textiles inscribed with ruler's names, which were often given as robes of honor, or also in larger pieces that could be tailored later (Munroe 2012).

Tiraz was highly valued and hence often stockpiled for later use. Even previously worn *tiraz* was kept and given out as favors, for instance in Fatimid Egypt (Sanders 2001). A jacket now in the collection of the Textile Museum was made in the Saljuq period from an earlier, Buyid period *tiraz* curtain; this transformation shows both the reuse value of such textiles, and the fact that *tiraz* could be used for furnishing purposes as well as dress (Winter 2020).[11] Surviving examples of ceremonial *tiraz* are rare, and often fragmentary (Figure 42). The donning of robes of honor, made of *tiraz*, was part of court ceremonies in which the recipient would put on the robe in front of a large audience. A famous image of such as in a scene appears in the *Jami' al-Tavarikh,* a universal history written by the Ilkhanid vizier Rashid al-Din (d. 1318) and copied multiple times in Arabic and Persian as a means to spread the Ilkhanids' view of history across the parts of the Islamic world they had come to rule (Hillenbrand 2011). In the image, Mahmud ibn Sebuktegin of Ghazni (r. 998–1030) receives a robe sent by the Abbasid caliph al-Qadir bi-llah (r. 991–1031), and is shown in the process of putting it on (Figure 43). The scene was included in the *Jami' al-Tavarikh* as a reference to Mahmud's importance as the patron of Firdowsi (d. 1025), the author of the *Shahnameh*, one of the major works of Persian literature that was highly admired at the Ilkhanid court in Iran. The first surviving illustrated manuscripts of the *Shahnameh* also date to the Ilkhanid period

---

[11] https://de1.zetcom-group.de/MpWeb-mpWashingtonGeoWashUniv/v?mode=online& objectId=22548.

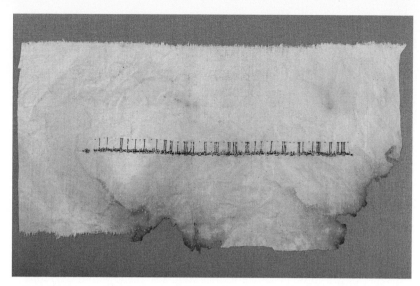

Figure 42 Tiraz textile fragment Egypt, date: 916–917: Al-Muqtadir (r. 907–933), Abbasid dynasty glazed linen tabby embroidered in silk. Dimensions: 21.6 × 40.6 cm; mount dimensions L. 28.5 × W. 49 cm. Royal Ontario Museum, Toronto. Object number: 978.76.42. Abemayor collection given in memory of Dr. Veronika Gervers, Associate Curator, Textile department (1968–1979) by Albert and Federico Friedberg. Image courtesy of the Royal Ontario Museum.

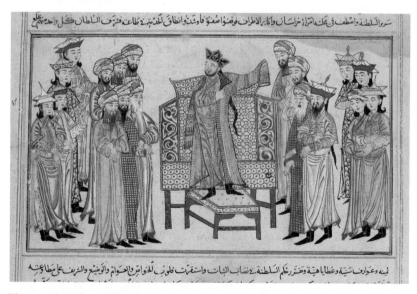

Figure 43 Mahmud ibn Sebuktegin, ruler of the Ghaznavid dynasty of eastern Afghanistan from 998–1030, receiving a robe of honor from the caliph al-Qadir Bi'llah. Rashid al-Din, *Jami' al-Tavarikh,* Iran, 1306 or 1314–15. Dimensions: 5.09 cm × 33.56 cm. Materials: Opaque watercolor, ink, gold, and silver on paper. Edinburgh University Library, or.ms. 20, fol. 121 r. Digital image: Copyright The University of Edinburgh. Original: Copyright The University of Edinburgh. Free use.

(Grabar and Blair 1980). The practice of gifting robes of honor spread throughout the medieval Islamic world, and also impacted court dress and practices in regions such as Armenia and Georgia (Eastmond and Jones 2001). Robes of honor thus were not exclusive to the Islamic world, but rather existed across medieval and early modern Eurasia (chapters in Gordon 2001).

For the most part, the production of *tiraz* was limited to authorized court workshops. At times, however, imitations of such textiles were made, for instance in Fatimid Egypt in the tenth to twelfth centuries, where an industry of producing *tiraz*-like textiles that were often used as burial shrouds developed (Sanders 2001; Sokoly 1997). Such textiles appeared in nonelite graves, and not only those of Muslims. *Tiraz*-like textiles were also made with inscriptions in Coptic (Figure 44) and Hebrew, in addition to Arabic (Dospěl Williams 2022). Extant examples of robes of honor are exceedingly rare, and most examples that

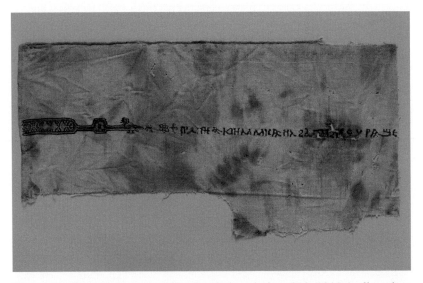

Figure 44 Three fragments with a Coptic inscription, 810–1010 (radiocarbon date, 95 percent probability). Attributed to Egypt, Akhmim (former Panopolis). Medium: Tapestry weave in polychrome and undyed wool on plain-weave ground of undyed wool; a row of stitches in undyed wool below the top edge. Dimensions: Textile fragment A: H. 31.4 cm (24 13/16 in.) × W. 63 × 31.4 cm (12 3/8 in.); Textile fragment B: H. 17.1 cm (6 3/4 in.) × W. 27.9 cm (11 in.); Textile fragment C: H. 31.6 cm (12 7/16 in.) × W. 52.7 cm (20 3/4 in.). Metropolitan Museum of Art, New York, Gift of George F. Baker, 1890, accession number: 90.5.877. Open access CC0.

do survive date to the early modern period, especially ones made in the Ottoman Empire (Phillips 2021).

As noted previously, medieval elite and court dress often survives in funerary settings. In Islamic contexts, however, the common practice of burying the dead wrapped only in large (usually linen) shrouds, without clothing underneath, means that very little such clothing still exists, although some has been found in archaeological contexts, in cases where the normative prescriptions were disregarded (see discussion specific to Egypt Section 5.3). Examples are few, and do not include full outfits, and so we have to rely on book painting, and ceramics such as twelfth-century *mina'i* ceramics from Iran that show detailed figural scenes, to get a sense of what men and women at medieval Islamic courts wore. A few examples of early modern kaftans for men and children exist in the Ottoman context, where they were preserved in Topkapi Palace as mementoes of sultans and princes (Ertuğ 1996; Tezcan 2006). For women's and girls' dress, however, little survives before the eighteenth century (Phillips 2021); for the eighteenth and nineteenth centuries, rich collections of such clothing exist at the Benaki Museum in Athens and the Sadberk Hanım Museum in Istanbul.

5.3 Elite Dress beyond the Royal Courts

In China, there is a long history of distinguishing between "northern" and "southern" dress that parallels ideas about the types of cloth produced north and south of the Yangtze River discussed in Section 3.3. As with the production of specific types of cloth, what people wore in the north and the south were more complex than this geographical distinction would suggest. In the north of China, which borders the steppe and Central Asia, interactions with groups of people such as the Xianbei, Sogdians, Uyghurs, Tangut, Tibetans, Khitan, Jurchen, and Mongols, among others, impacted the types of clothing people wore. These groups were by and large adept equestrians, some were nomadic or semi-nomadic, and most had long and culturally important hunting traditions. While the specifics of their dress differed, all of these groups wore some variation of a fitted riding coat, belted, with trousers and boots. This "northern" style of dress was worn by the Chinese in the sixth century in some contexts, with both women and men wearing variations of a fitted riding coat, trousers, and boots (Chen 2019; Lingley 2010). In addition, "southern" forms of dress, such as long flowing sleeves and robes, and cropped jackets, were adopted by men at the Khitan court in the tenth century for specific courtly occasions. Meaning was conveyed by different forms of dress, and historical evidence shows that elites could partake in forms of cultural code switching by donning one form of dress or another in certain contexts.

The Sogdians stand out from these other groups as they were not native north China or Mongolia, but to Sogdiana, an area that encompassed present-day Uzbekistan and Tajikistan. They played an essential role as cultural intermediaries and lived in communities along the Silk Road such as the oasis towns skirting the Taklamakan desert and had a substantial presence in Chang'an. Evidence for Sogdian dress and their religious practices in China are found in the imagery adorning stone-cut and painted funerary couches made for the tombs of community leaders, called *sabao*, such as An Jia and Shi Jun (Wirkak) in the sixth century. These funerary couches memorialize the *sabao* wearing northern-style dress, while his wife is depicted in Chinese-style dress. The Sogdians were also likely responsible for the spread of the pearl roundel motif, although its origin is a matter of some debate (Gasparini 2019). Pictorial evidence for the pearl roundel exists in the tomb of the Xianbei noble Xu Xianxiu (dated 571) in Shanxi Province, China as well as in the late Sasanian rock-cut reliefs of Taq e-Bustan (ca. fourth century, Kermanshah Province, Iran). The mural paintings of banqueting Sogdian merchants from Panjikent (present-day Tajikistan) and Afrasiab (present-day Uzbekistan) also feature the distinctive pearl roundel (Compareti 2003). This motif was also favored by Tang dynasty elites and is represented on funerary figures (Chen 2019). Extant silk samite fragments from China are also important evidence for this popular motif; survivals of fragments of Sasanian and Sasanian-imitation silk textiles found in grave contexts in Antinoë and in western European church treasuries further demonstrate the geographically expansive reach of the design type (Calament and Durand 2013; Canepa 2014; Jeroussalimskaja 1993). Typically woven in polychrome samite, the pearl roundel usually features an animal motif surrounded by the characteristic pearls. The pattern of confronted ducks on split palmettes, as in the child's coat discussed Section 3.3 (see Figure 26), is a well-preserved example of this pattern.

In the Mediterranean context in this same time period, evidence for noncourt dress is again biased toward Egypt because of the area's dry climate. Thousands of textiles were preserved in Egyptian graves dating from the late Roman through Mamluk periods, including both dress and furnishing textiles, in graves belonging to Christians and Muslims from a range of social classes (see Section 6 for discussion of furnishing textiles). However, it is only in recent years that these sites have been scientifically excavated to provide data points that might help identify not only wearers but also specific cultural aspects of dress practice. Although Egyptian tunic shapes and decorative motifs changed over the centuries from the late antique through Islamic eras, a few

Figure 45 Tunic with Dionysian ornament. Probably fifth century. Said to be from Egypt, Akhmim (former Panopolis). Medium: Linen, wool; plain weave, tapestry weave. Dimensions: Tunic: L. 183 cm (72 1/16 in.) × W. 135 cm (53 1/8 in.). Metropolitan Museum of Art, New York, Gift of Edward S. Harkness, 1926, accession number: 26.9.8. Open access CC0.

commonalities can be traced out (Pritchard 2006; Rooijakkers 2017). Egyptian tunics tended to feature decorative elements that highlighted the structural elements of the human body: decorations clustered at the neckline, at the opening of the sleeve, along the bottom edge of the garment (*orbiculi*), and over the shoulders (*clavi*). One can discern changing tastes for dress styles over time, not only in the imagery represented on garments but also in the color palette used and in the style of the individual designs. Earlier tunics tended toward undyed linen grounds with monochromatic details in tapestry weave (Figure 45), while later examples increasingly deployed colorful grounds and elaborate iconographic details entirely in wool tapestry weave (Figure 46). There appears to be little differentiation in the gender of dress in this period, apart perhaps from the size of the tunics; children's tunics (Figure 47) essentially replicated the styles of adult tunics, but in smaller dimensions (Kwaspen and Verhecken-Lammens 2015). There are also numerous tunics with fuzzy pile on the inside of the garment, a detail adding coziness and protection against the cold (Figure 48).

Figure 46 Tunic, c. 670–870, Egypt. Medium: Plain-woven wool, with appliqué ornaments tapestry-woven in colored wool and linen on linen warps. Dimensions: Height 131 cm, including sleeve width: 209 cm, excluding sleeve width: 124 cm. Victoria and Albert Museum, London, inv. no. 2275–1891 to 303–1891 © Victoria and Albert Museum, London.

Figure 47 Child's tunic with hood, 600–900, attributed to Egypt, tapestry weave in purple-colored, red-brown, and undyed wool on plain-weave ground of green wool; fringes in green and red-brown along the perimeter of the hood and lower edges. Dimensions: (including sleeves and hood) H. 89.1 cm (35 1/16 in.) × W. 101 cm (39 3/4 in.). Metropolitan Museum of Art, New York, Gift of George D. Pratt, 1927, accession number: 27.239. Open access CC0.

Figure 48 Tunic, sixth–seventh century, attributed to Egypt, Akhmim (former Panopolis). Medium: Linen, wool, and silk. Dimensions: H. 102.9 cm (40 1/2 in.) × W. 157.5 cm (62 in.). Metropolitan Museum of Art, New York, Gift of George F. Baker, 1890, accession number: 90.5.901. Open access CC0.

Generally speaking, Egyptian tunics in the late Roman, Byzantine, and early Islamic periods were woven as integral pieces of cloth with minimal stitching (Colburn 2016). Weavers focused instead on the drape of the garment, which could be modified by changing the proportions of different elements (such as narrow arms or shortened hems) or introducing additional elements like belts and tucks. These details are difficult to appreciate in current museum storage or display, where tunics, often fragmentary, are displayed inert in cases or in drawers, generally spread out and laid flat in a way that is beneficial for preservation (since fragile textiles can break at fold lines). Such conditions make it challenging to imagine how garments once looked on the human body. Replicas and reconstructions[12] of such garments, however, help modern viewers appreciate how people of the period played with drapery, shape, and volume, even layering different garments to create a bulky, puffy effect (Calamant and Durand 2013).

Visual and textual sources can be added to these surviving material examples to give a more complete sense of dress practice around the early medieval Mediterranean. Documentary sources from late antique Egypt, for example, suggest that tunics were not only made to order but were also handed down or traded on a secondary market. Evidence of ancient repairs and alterations supports the idea that tunics were prized possessions to be mended and worn

---

[12] www.youtube.com/watch?v=-cdhnORIAvo.

until threadbare. It is likely that people owned only a few garments in their lifetime. In addition, the study of dress assemblages — not only tunics but also accompanying accessories like headgear, shoes, jewelry, and the like — can shed light on new questions about the relationship of dress and individual and communal identity in a period when Egypt underwent significant cultural changes in the centuries of transformation from pre-Christian to Islamic rule (Pleşa 2017).

Textual sources are also helpful in understanding dress practices in the medieval Mediterranean. The documents preserved in the Cairo Geniza are especially valuable in this regard. These fragmentary sources, discovered in the storeroom of a medieval synagogue in Fustat, convey information about the activities of numerous Jewish communities around the medieval Mediterranean and beyond (Goitein 1983; Goitein and Friedman 2007). Dowry lists, for example, include lists of household possessions and dress items, and many of these list household textiles at length. Some feature unusual names associated with other locales, such as Sicily, suggesting the multidirectional movement of finished garments or fashions from one region to another along trade and travel routes. These documentary texts can be read alongside literary works such as the *Kitab al-Muwashsha* (The Brocade Book), an Abbasid period literary text that carefully describes the most current fashionable dress styles in ninth-century Baghdad, most prominently inscribed garments (al-Washsha, trans. Bouhlal 2004). These textual sources point to a multiregional network of dress fashion, as styles in one area came to be emulated in another.

Visual evidence further bolsters our understanding of the interconnected nature of fashionable dress practices around the Mediterranean. Jennifer Ball has observed such interregional trends in her study on Byzantine dress, arguing that court centers like Constantinople were likely recipients of dress fashions percolating in border zones that were imported back into the capital, an observation that disrupts center-periphery models of the movement of fashionable dress (Ball 2005). A twelfth-century representation of Anna Radene in a church in Kastoria, Greece, for example, depicts a finely attired woman wearing elaborate earrings, a fashionable cap, and several layers of fine textiles, ostensibly imported silks because of their repeating patterns. The image visualizes the multidirectional movement of dress styles and changing, interregional fashions that typified the dress of nonruling elites in the medieval Mediterranean (Figure 49).

Beyond the elite context, further rules existed for the types of garments and fabrics that certain parts of the population were allowed to use and wear. In the Islamic world, sumptuary rules for Muslims regarded three major points: the use of silk; the use of fabric with figural patterns; and the use of certain colors. Wearing silk was discouraged especially for men, and more so for undergarments

Figure 49 Wall painting showing Anna Radene, Byzantine church of Aghioi Anargyroi, Kastoria, twelfth century. By permission of the Ephorate of Antiquities at Kastoria. © Hellenic Ministry of Culture and Sports/ Archaeological Receipts Fund.

than for exterior clothing, although attitudes varied among the four Sunni schools of Islamic law (Levy-Rubin 2011: 130–132). Mixed fabrics that contained silk were considered less problematic than pure silk. As a rule, shrouds were not made of silk, but rather of linen (Baker 1995: 16–17). Textiles with figural images were considered less problematic when used for furnishings such as cushions or curtains, and some more reluctance was applied to these fabrics for clothing, at least in Sunni contexts. White was a preferred color for men's clothing because of its mention in a *hadith* (tradition associated with the Prophet Muhammad) associated with Paradise. Black and blue were colors of mourning, while red had over time varying associations, both positive and negative. Different laws applied for *dhimmi*s, that is members of Jewish, Christian and other communities living under Muslim rule, all ultimately rules aimed at visibly othering non-Muslims in the public space (Stillman 2000: 101–119). Various colors such as yellow, red, and black could be prescribed for their street clothing, as could the wearing of specific badges, or requirements for haircuts, and prohibitions on using horses for transport, along with rules for religious practice in public (Baker 1995: 17; Emon 2012: 131–136; Levy-Rubin 2011: 146–162). *Dhimmi*s were, for instance, not allowed to wear *tiraz* (Levy-Rubin 2011: 148). This prohibition, however, was limited to court-produced *tiraz*. Innumerable inscribed textiles were made in commercial workshops, some featuring Hebrew and Coptic inscriptions (see Figure 44) in addition to Arabic ones, indicating their popular use among Jewish and Christian customers as well (Dospěl Williams 2022). Surviving examples of Coptic-inscribed textiles, for instance, feature biblical verses evoking divine protection and

Figure 50 Major Sakkos of Metropolitan Photios, probably after 1408 and before 1417, pearls re-strung 1631 and 1642. Medium/technique: Silk and silver-gilt thread embroidery and pearls on satin, buttons and silver bells, taffeta lining. Dimensions: H. 135 × W. 123 cm (H. 53.1 × W. 48.4 in.). Kremlin Museums, Moscow, inv. no. TK-4. Photographer: V. V. Blagov. © State Historical and Cultural Museum and Heritage Site "The Moscow Kremlin." Licensee Patricia Blessing 2023.

recalling spiritual struggle, suggesting they may have had magical functions or have reflected Coptic Christians' broader attitudes about their position in Muslim society (Van der Vliet 2006).

Surviving textiles from the late Byzantine period attest to the splendor of ecclesiastical dress and liturgical furnishings in the later Middle Ages (Woodfin 2010, 2012). The *sakkos*, a heavy garment signifying the authority of bishops, was a liturgical garment made of luxurious silk, densely decorated with sacred imagery in exquisite embroidery, and covered with gemstones and pearls, as in the Major *Sakkos* of

Figure 51 Fragment of a vestment, Bursa? Constantinople? sixteenth century. Technique/material: Silk and gilt-metal-strip-wrapped silk, warp-float faced satin weave with weft-float faced twill interlacings of secondary binding warp and supplementary patterning weft. Dimensions: H. 68.7 × W. 42.0 cm (27 1/16 × 16 9/16 in.). © Byzantine Collection, Dumbarton Oaks Research Library and Collection, BZ.1952.10.

Metropolitan Photios (Figure 50), made in the early fifteenth century (Bogdanović 2014; Woodfin 2012: 122–126). The *epitaphios*, a liturgical furnishing decorated with a depiction of the dead body of Christ that is used in Orthodox Holy Saturday matins, received similarly ornate embellishment in its most spectacular examples (Woodfin 2004). By the late Byzantine period, workshops in Constantinople and Bursa were also producing high-end figural silks depicting religious scenes in small repeats, including representations of Christ in a gesture of blessing or the symbols of the Evangelists; this weaving tradition would continue into the Ottoman and Safavid period in Armenian communities (Figure 51). Today, many extraordinary late Byzantine textiles trace their provenance through Orthodox monastic communities, such as Mount Athos, where they arrived as commissions or imperial gifts. They are often preserved alongside textiles from the Islamic world, pointing again to the complex networks along which luxury textiles traveled in the late medieval Middle East, Mediterranean, and Eastern Europe (Sullivan 2021; Vryzidis 2019a, 2019b, 2020).

6 Furnishing Textiles

Beyond uses for clothing — perhaps the most obvious presence of textiles in the contemporary reader's life — various kinds of fabrics were used to furnish spaces. Such objects range from carpets and curtains to wall-hangings and pillows. While many such textiles could be used in both religious and domestic settings, others had more specific functions — for instance prayer rugs in the Islamic world, altar cloths in churches, and curtains for Torah shrines in synagogues. A challenge presented in studying such objects within their spatial contexts is that they frequently have been preserved in museum collections, often without their original purpose known, and at times with changed shapes because of dealer interventions or conservation practices. Both issues reflect historical reuse, on the one hand, and nineteenth-century collecting practices, on the other hand.

   The fragmentation of textiles in these conditions has significantly hampered their integration into discussions of medieval interiors (Bühl et al. 2019; Stephenson 2014). Apart from pieces of exceptional size, it is often challenging to securely identify scraps of surviving textiles as belonging to furnishing textiles. The isometric drawings common in many art and architectural history textbooks, for example, are usually depicted devoid of furnishings of any kind, which deemphasizes the singular importance of textiles in medieval homes, churches, palaces, synagogues, mosques, and the other buildings to affect the visual and sensorial experience of space. One reason is because furnishing textiles rarely survive in situ; in reality, they are generally found in other circumstances, including

Figure 52 Palatium, Sant'Apollinare Nuovo, Ravenna, Italy. Photograph by Patricia Blessing, 2008. Reproduced by permission of Opera di Religione della Diocesi di Ravenna.

in tertiary use as grave wrappings. But visual sources commonly depict curtains and other furnishing textiles; the sixth-century wall mosaics of Sant'Apollinare Nuovo (ca. 504–561) in Ravenna, for example, show curtains fluttering in the arcade of the imperial palace with details including fringes, curtain rods, and loops (Figure 52). Curtain hooks have been preserved over the doors leading from narthex to naos in Hagia Sophia (Blessing 2018: fig. 9 and 10; Woodfin 2021: 594–595), but not the curtains themselves (Maguire 2019). Textual sources, too, list precious textiles like altar coverings, curtains, cushions, and the like as part of the fittings of churches from the smallest villages to the most important centers in Constantinople and Rome (Caseau 2007; Martiniani-Reber 1999).

Rare examples of floor coverings attest to the use of cut- and knotted pile carpets in the Eastern Mediterranean as well; the carbon-dating of such unique survivors has securely placed these early rugs in the late antique through early Islamic periods (Spuhler 2014). Some examples — such as a fourth- or fifth-century carpet at the Metropolitan Museum of Art (see Figure 3) — bear repeating geometric designs reminiscent of those seen in floor mosaics,[13] thus drawing attention to the multidirectional movement of motifs between architectural decors and furnishing fabrics. One particularly fascinating group of carpets (Figure 53) bears inscriptions naming their place and dates of production in Abbasid

---

[13] http://museum.doaks.org/objects-1/info/35763.

Figure 53 Tiraz, Egypt; Akhmim, 818–819. Linen and wool. Dimensions: L. 31.75 × W. 36.83 cm (L. 12 1/2 × W. 14 1/2 in.). Structure: Supplementary weft-loop pile; plain weave, warp-predominant. The Textile Museum Collection, The Textile Museum, Washington, DC, inv.no. 73.726. Gift of Aziz S. Atiya in 1958.

Figure 54 General view of the so-called Dionysos hanging, fourth century, wool and linen, Dimensions: 210 cm (6 ft 10 5/8 in.) × 700 cm. (22 ft 11 1/2 in.). Abegg-Stiftung, CH-3132 Riggisberg, inv. no. 3100a. © Abegg-Stiftung, CH-3132 Riggisberg, 2015. Photo: Christoph von Viràg.

Akhmim, mentioned in early Islamic textual sources as a renowned production center for furnishing textiles (Theologou et al. 2008). Today these rare early carpets survive as mere fragments, deposited in their final use in graves to wrap, cover, or cushion bodies when too worn to have served as interior decoration.

Yet despite the scanty scholarship and interpretative challenges, furnishing textiles stand out as some of the most spectacular objects to survive from the medieval world. An almost twenty-three-foot long hanging of the ancient god

Figure 55 Large hanging. Egypt? Fourth century. Materials: Wool, linen. Dimensions: L. 213.40 × W. 117.00 cm (L. 84 1/32 × W. 46 1/16 in). The Textile Museum Collection, The Textile Museum, Washington, DC, acquired by George Hewitt Myers in 1925, inv. no. 71.18.

Dionysus and his retinue (Figure 54) dated to the fourth century, for example, depicts the figures in an arcade engaged in dancing, drinking, and merrymaking (Willers and Niekamp 2015). The sheer size of this textile (the figures themselves are just about life-size) points to the enormous dimensions of its original setting. Textiles like this often make reference to the architectural spaces they once adorned, featuring various elements like columns and arcades as part of their design. A fourth-century hanging depicting a pair of columns and jeweled pediment, for example, portrays a verdant garden populated with birds suggesting a fictive space beyond the picture frame (Figure 55). The design logic of these textiles suggests a taste for layering textiles over real architectural elements like columns, walls, and arcades, perhaps for special occasions or celebrations to impress guests. In this sense, these examples bring up a crucial point when considering medieval furnishing textiles more generally, namely their role in shaping space, often in a temporary, or infinitely modifiable, manner (Weddigen 2013).

Furnishing textiles also suggest the blurring of lines between domestic and public spaces, and secular and sacred contexts. Furnishing textiles sharing iconographic themes may have been used in multiple contexts, and these uses may have changed over time. A sixth-century hanging depicting the ancient goddess Hestia on a jeweled throne with attendants, for example, shares many iconographic similarities with a contemporary hanging of the Virgin surrounded by angels. The parallels have led scholars to suggest that the works represent overlapping traditions of pre-Christian and Christian imagery and practices well into the early medieval period (Figure 56 and Figure 57). On closer comparison, however, numerous stylistic, technical, and iconographic differences — such as the quality of the weaving, the colors of the underlying warps, preferences for outlining in black, and the overall representation of depth — suggest these objects should be seen as representing separate workshop traditions and possibly even cultural contexts. The iconic quality of the Virgin and the image's strong emphasis on frontality, for example, suggest this work meant to be viewed at distance and from straight on. The weavers in the Hestia hanging, in contrast, play

Figure 56 Hanging with Hestia Polyolbus. Egypt, ca. sixth century. Dimensions: H. (weft) 114.5 cm × W. (warp) 138.0 cm (45 1/16 × 54 5/16 in.). Medium/technique: Tapestry weave in polychrome wool. © Byzantine Collection, Dumbarton Oaks Research Library and Collection, Washington, DC, BZ.1929.1.

Figure 57 Icon of the Virgin and Child, 500s, Egypt, Byzantine period, sixth century. Medium/technique: Slit-and dovetailed-tapestry weave; wool. Dimensions: Overall – 178.7 × 110.5 cm (70 3/8 × 43 1/2 in.); mounted: 197.4 × 128.2 × 6.4 cm (77 11/16 × 50 1/2 × 2 1/2 in.). Cleveland Museum of Art, Cleveland, Leonard C. Hanna, Jr. Fund, 1967.144. Open access CC0.

up the depth of the background foliage and set her deeply in her throne, resulting in visual effects that invite a more intimate viewing experience. That Hestia survives incomplete because the textile was cut to its current niche shape at some point on the art market only heightens the mystery of her original use. We are left wondering whether the goddess of the hearth was intended for a domestic setting, while the Virgin for a more public context, such as a church, or whether the portability of the textiles meant they could have had a whole range of uses. The comparison of these examples demonstrates the challenges art historians face when studying furnishing textiles in absence of complete surviving fragments discovered in situ with clear information about use.

Furnishing textiles are also challenging to interpret today because of the multiple functions a single fabric might have served over the course of its useful lifetime. Curtains, for example, may have had multiple functions in a home, serving to block off doors, divide up rooms, delineate bed space, insulate walls, or other shifting functions according to need (Parani 2019). In Byzantine and Islamic imperial and caliphal courts, for example, silk curtains were used as a device for enhancing the dramatic hiding and revealing of the emperor and caliph as part of highly choreographed ceremonies (Featherstone 2005; Sanders 1994; Shalem 2006). But identifying textiles today as clearly having once served as curtains in this manner is very challenging, as apart from loops along the tops of the fabric, it is nearly impossible to tell (Colburn 2019).

For the medieval Islamic world, two curtains now held in the collection of the Cleveland Museum of Art have long been associated with the Alhambra, the fourteenth-century palace of the Nasrids in Granada (Figure 58). Like for many objects associated with the Alhambra, these curtains do not have a clear provenance to the site, indicating that they were indeed removed from there. Thus, the connection to the site is made based on stylistic observations that connect the motifs used on the fabric to similar ones that appear on the architectural decoration of the Alhambra, particularly in its rich stucco decoration. In a detailed study of the Alhambra, Olga Bush has argued for the central role that textiles played within the spaces of the palace, and has shown how sources dating to the fourteenth century describe the use of textiles — from pillows to entire tents — within the space for specific ceremonies (Bush 2018). Such uses are hard to imagine on site today, since no historical objects remain in it apart from fountain basins, some in modern copies.

Therefore, the so-called Alhambra curtains encompass two major problems in the study of furnishing textiles: first, the fact that most such objects are no longer present in their original contexts; and second, the presentation of these textiles in museum contexts as objects per se, divorced from their original surroundings. Such observations are especially true for palaces that were often abandoned centuries ago, if they even still exist as structures that can be visited as museums (such as the Alhambra, the Alcazar in Seville, or Topkapı Palace in Istanbul). But they are also true for many religious monuments that are still used in their original function today. Take the examples of mosques: these spaces were always furnished with rugs covering the floors for the comfort and hygiene of worshippers who bow down low on the ground during prayers. Yet the carpets found in historical mosques across the Islamic world today are rarely contemporary to the buildings themselves. Carpets were often exchanged multiple times over the centuries, renewed as existing ones were damaged due to extensive use; after all, worshippers coming into a mosque five times per day, walking through the space, and kneeling on the carpets would have

Figure 58 Silk curtain from the Alhambra palace, 1300s, Spain, Granada, Nasrid period. Medium: Lampas and taqueté, silk. Dimensions: Overall – 438.2 × 271.8 cm (172 1/2 × 107 in.). Cleveland Museum of Art, Cleveland, Leonard C. Hanna, Jr. Fund 1982.16. Open access CC0.

caused wear and tear, even though shoes are not worn inside mosques. In some cases, historical carpets were removed in the nineteenth century, some looted and sold off on the art market, some taken into local museums for safekeeping following thefts at other sites. Such is the case of the Museum of Turkish and Islamic Art in Istanbul today, which grew out of attempts by the Ottoman authorities beginning in the late nineteenth century to preserve objects (such as carpets, candle sticks, and Qur'an manuscripts) from religious sites across the Ottoman Empire after many had been stolen (Eldem 2016). The museum's collection of carpets from Anatolia, dating from the thirteenth to the seventeenth centuries, is extensive (Denny and Krody 2002: 15–55).

Textile furnishings are connected to the broader context of textile architectures, or textile as architecture (Blessing 2018; Ekici et al. 2023). This includes objects such as canopies or tents. While such textile architecture is often depicted in paintings produced by many of the cultures covered in this Element, the objects themselves have rarely been preserved. Sometimes, such objects were later reworked into clothing or liturgical garments. Such is the case of the Fermo Chasuble, a liturgical garment that was created from a piece of fabric originally used as a canopy as a recent, extensive research and conservation project has demonstrated (Shalem 2017). Objects that saw heavy use, especially tents that

Figure 59 Tomb occupant couple seated beside a table. Dimensions: Height 92 cm, width 132 cm. Zhao Daweng's tomb, Baisha Henan, 1099 CE, after Su Bai, *Baisha Song mu* (Beijing: Wenwu chubanshe, 2002), plate 5.

Figure 60 Left half of a lampas-woven textile, silk, gilded paper, and gilded animal substrate. China or the Eastern Islamic area. First half of fourteenth century. Dimensions: Height 228, width 63.5 cm. The David Collection, Copenhagen, 40/1997, photograph: Pernille Klemp.

Figure 61 Panel with phoenixes and flowers. Yuan dynasty (1271–1368).
Fourteenth century, China. Medium/technique: Silk and metallic thread embroidery
on silk gauze. Dimensions: Overall – 143.2 × 134.6 cm (56 3/8 × 53 in.); mount: 154
× 146.3 × 7.6 cm (60 5/8 × 57 5/8 × 3 in.), Metropolitan Museum of Art, New York,
Purchase, Amalia Lacroze de Fortabat Gift, Louis V. Bell and Rogers Funds, and
Lita Annenberg Hazen Charitable Trust Gift, in honor of Ambassador Walter
H. Annenberg, 1988, accession number: 1988.82. Open access CC0.

Figure 62 Tile with image of phoenix, late thirteenth century, Iran, probably
Takht-i Sulayman, stonepaste; modeled, underglaze painted in blue and
turquoise, luster-painted on opaque white ground. Dimensions: Height 37.5 cm
(14 3/4 in.), width 36.2 cm (14 1/4 in.). Metropolitan Museum of Art,
New York, Rogers Fund, 1912, accession number: 12.49.4. Open access CC0.

were used outside in all kinds of weather, and taken on military campaigns, have rarely survived. In the Islamic world, the earliest extant examples are Ottoman military tents from the seventeen and eighteenth centuries (Dimmig 2016) and eighteenth-century ones from South Asia (Chowdhury 2015). Some of the techniques that are still used to produce appliqué tents and home decor in Egypt today date back to the medieval and early modern period, but no examples that predate the nineteenth century survive today (El Rashidi and Bowker 2018: 1–80).

Textiles played a major role in furnishing the interior spaces in China, but the evidence for such textiles and how they were used is often lacking. Although some articles have been preserved in the funerary context, their original use in above ground interior spaces must be extrapolated from the surviving pictorial evidence. Curtains, screens, hangings, tablecloths, pillows, mats, and carpets are variously depicted in the painted tombs of the tenth through fourteenth centuries during the Liao, Jin, Song, and Yuan dynasties. For example, in the occupant portrait of a husband-and-wife couple in Zhao Dawang's tombs in Baishan, Henan, from 1099, curtains are visible at the top of the painting, with screens depicting a wave motif behind each of the occupants (Figure 59). During the Yuan dynasty, the Mongol rulers of China constructed permanent architecture and cities, but preferred to continue to dwell and hold court audiences in tents. Tents used by Mongol rulers could be enormous, and the interiors were sometimes clad in gold-woven lampas panels (al-Din trans. Thackston 1998–99; Wardwell 1998–99). Examples of Mongol gold-woven tent panels are now in several museum collections around the world (Figure 60). Patterns and motifs found on textiles such as confronted birds in roundels, or encircling phoenixes were imitated in permanent architecture. For example, a fourteenth-century canopy showing phoenixes circling a pearl (Figure 61) is similar to a stone relief panel found near Beijing from this period. The East Asian phoenix was also used to adorn glazed tiles serving as revetment for Ilkhanid imperial structures such as the palace at Takht-i Sulayman (c. 1270) and elsewhere in Iran (Figure 62), reflecting the use of such motifs within the context of the Mongol Empire as it expanded into the Islamic world (Kadoi 2009).

7 Imported Textiles in European Church Treasuries

European church treasuries represent some of the richest sites that preserve global medieval textiles even today. The range of fabrics preserved in monasteries and churches demonstrates Europe's connections around the Mediterranean, Middle East, and Asia. Many silks represent types not known from any other contexts, including especially rare examples of Sasanian,

Sogdian, and Byzantine silks (Oepen et al. 2011; Stauffer 2016). Though scholars have long posited that these textiles arrived in Europe as direct diplomatic gifts, in reality they featured in any number of exchanges from and through Central Asia, through Byzantium, and onwards to the Mediterranean, including interregional trade, local donations, and high-level exchanges (Dospěl Williams 2023; Luyster 2021). Influential individuals also undoubtedly played important roles in the movement of these textiles to their final repositories in Europe as well, particularly in the exchanges between Byzantium and the Abbasid caliphate with the Carolingian and Ottonian courts. The Byzantine princess Theophanu, for example, brought numerous luxurious items along with her upon her marriage to Otto II (r. 973–83); illuminations of her marriage charter dated 972 make visual allusion to imperial purple silks, suggesting these too also traveled with her (Garrison 2017).

Imported textiles in European treasuries also build on a longstanding tradition of wrapping sacred objects in fabric. In the Islamic world, the example of the *kiswa*, the textile cover wrapping the Kaaba stands out as a particularly salient example of this phenomenon (Shalem 2015). In the Christian context,

Figure 63 Fragment with eagles in roundels from the reliquary of Saint Librada in Siguenza Cathedral, 1100–50, Spain, Almería. Medium/technique: Silk and gold thread, lampas weave. Dimensions: Overall – 36.8 × 40.6 cm (14 1/2 × 16 in.); mount: 47 × 50.8 cm (18 1/2 × 20 in.); framed: 49.5 × 53.3 cm (19 1/2 × 21 in.). Cleveland Museum of Art, Cleveland. Purchase from the J. H. Wade Fund 1952.15. Open access CC0.

relics were frequently wrapped in textiles, often in several layers, before they were placed into shrines. As shrines were opened in later centuries, these wrappings were often removed, and in many cases divided up between museum collections. Textiles from the shrine of St. Librada in Siguenza (Spain), for instance, are now found in several collections, where they arrived through the art market after the shrine was opened in 1948. Fragments of two textiles, one with a griffin motif (Figure 63) and another with eagles, are thought to have been produced in Almería, from where they were taken after Alfonso VII conquered the city in 1147. While it was a longstanding practice to divide such wrappings, new conservation standards now aim at minimizing damage and to keep textiles intact as much as possible. A recent example is the restoration of the textiles from the twelfth-century shrine of Bishop Godehard (d. 1038) completed at the Abegg-Stiftung in Riggisberg, Switzerland (Schorta 2010). The opening of the shrine in 2010 was documented on video, and the textiles are now on view in the Dommuseum in Hildesheim, Germany.[14]

In some instances, precious imported textiles became relics in their new European contexts, taking on new meanings over time as the origins became obscured or reimagined (Rosser-Owen 2015) . For example, a large format, red silk of the tenth century depicting elephants in enormous roundels is one of the very few that can be securely linked to Byzantine imperial production, thanks to a Greek inscription along its bottom edge. It provides the names and court titles of two individuals, including the *archon*, a certain Peter, the official responsible for controlling its production in a Constantinopolitan palace workshop (Muthesius 1997). The fabric was buried with Charlemagne in Aachen before being "rediscovered" when his tomb was reopened centuries after his death; it subsequently came to be honored as if a relic in its own right (Figure 64). Another example, the so-called "Veil of Saint Anne,"[15] today held in the Cathedral Treasury of Apt, France, follows this same trend. The textile features Arabic inscriptions in silk and metallic thread naming its production in the *tiraz al-khassa* (private caliphal *tiraz* factory) of Damietta in the tenth century, during the rule of the Fatimid caliph al-Musta'li (r. 1094–1101). Although the precise path this textile took to arrive in Apt is unclear, it is possible it was looted and brought there in the wake of the Crusades, following the same fate of many luxury objects brought from Byzantium and Fatimid territories to Europe (Brubaker 2004).

---

[14] www.youtube.com/watch?v=T9Qyxk5s3DY.
[15] www.qantara-med.org/public/show_document.php?do_id=1115&lang=en.

Figure 64 Elephant silk, tenth century, Byzantium. Aachen, Germany, Treasury of the Cathedral. Photograph by Alamy.

The designation of such textiles as relics may seem curious today; indeed, it is at odds with today's art historical methodologies that seek to attribute textiles to specific dates and places of production. Yet medieval Europeans' understanding of objects was complex and even circular in its logic: a textile might be perceived simultaneously as representative of current production while retaining the aura of a historical artifact. Indeed, in the case of textiles, it was sometimes enough that the fabric was sourced from the Holy Land or contained Arabic script for it to become associated with the biblical past (Nagel 2011). Europeans understood that such fabrics were sourced in contemporaneous production centers in the Middle East or Asia as trade items, loot, or diplomatic gifts, but they saw no contradiction in understanding that something produced recently could stand in as representative of older types (Mack 2001: 52–56). We see a similar trend playing out also in Italian panel paintings of the late medieval period: there, depictions of holy figures, particularly the Virgin, show the figures wearing near contemporary *tiraz*, suggesting both an appreciation for luxury imported textiles and a complete disregard for the realities of time and space (Schulz 2018). A fifteenth-century painting of the Adoration of the Magi by Gentile da Fabriano, for example, depicts a crowd of figures in luxurious contemporary dress, including a nursemaid to the left wearing garments inscribed with repeating bands of Arabic and a groom in an Arabic-inscribed sash leading a horse (Figure 65).

Figure 65 Gentile da Fabriano, Adoration of the Magi, 1423, tempera on wood. Dimensions: 300 × 282 cm. Uffizi, Florence, inv. 1890 no. 8364. Photograph: Uffizi.

8 Aesthetics

Over the centuries examined here, aesthetic value was a major concern in the production, sale, appreciation, use, and reuse of textiles. It is also true that the more intricate and valuable (from a material and aesthetic point of view) textiles were, the more likely they were to have been preserved. Thus, essential items of clothing such as stockings, underwear, shirts, and cloaks that were made of linen, wool, or cotton depending on climate, were much less likely to have been preserved, also because daily use would have eventually rendered them unusable. Even in periods when clothing was regularly mended, rather than discarded at the first rip or tear, there was a limit to what could be fixed. Precious fabrics, even in court contexts, were much less likely to have been worn on a daily basis. Especially rich items of clothing such as those in the thirteenth- and fourteenth-century royal tombs of the Monastery of Santa María la Real de las Huelgas in Burgos, Spain, were reserved for ceremonial occasions (Feliciano 2005). Liturgical vestments used by priests and bishops in Christian contexts changed according to the liturgical calendar, with some vestments reserved for specific feast days, and so not heavily used. As such, the material record is inevitably skewed, even when taking into account the rare survivals of simpler garments, for instance the undergarments from the Las Huelgas tombs. Reuse of textiles, such as in Christian reliquaries as discussed Section 7, had both aesthetic and historical components. Thus, a textile could be reused in a shrine because it was associated with a particular saint, such as Saint Isidore in Leon whose eleventh-century reliquary contains earlier textiles associated with the translation of the relics from Seville (Cabrera Lafuente 2020; Feliciano 2020). Here, memory is embedded in the use of textiles. Yet such textiles were also considered beautiful, and therefore could also be reused in settings where they were visible, such as liturgical vestments that were often retailored over time (and even into the early modern period) to fit new conventions for these garments, while the older textiles were retained (Borkopp-Restle 2019).

What, then, were some of the aesthetic considerations behind the ways in which people chose and appreciated textiles? For silk, its sheen and light weight was a major draw. Thus, in the context of Abbasid Iraq in the ninth century, shimmering silk was one of the items that carried the desired effect called *buqalamun*, which refers to scintillating, changing color. This effect could be held by natural materials such as peacock feathers or mother of pearl as much as by human-made ones such as textiles or luster ceramics, and was part of the wider aesthetics of *'ajab* (wonder, in Arabic) that was highly prized (Saba 2012). Textiles were ideally suited to an aesthetic framework interested in notions of instability embodied in changing visual effects, and in objects made to intentionally confuse the viewer, who could never be quite sure what, for instance, the color of an object was. Silk could do this, both on plain weaves and even more so as damask, in which a pattern is woven in a single color and becomes more or less visible depending on lighting. Brocaded fabrics, with gold threads woven into them, could provide this glittering effect even more efficiently.

While the aesthetics of *'ajab* were particularly well-developed in the medieval Islamic world, similar ideas were also appreciated in other contexts. Thus, both Arabic poetry and Greek poetry from the Byzantine period engage with shimmering and glittering effects as an effect to be appreciated (Pentcheva 2015). In late antiquity, the joining of glittering gemstones and textiles could take various forms. Of course, rich textiles could be worn together with equally luxurious jewelry, such as in the mosaic of Theodora and her retinue in Ravenna (see Figure 37). But motifs imitating jewelry could also be woven into textiles, which in turn could be worn together with jewelry, creating layers of material and meaning (Dospĕl Williams 2018b). In addition, silks' repeating patterns — an inherent aspect of the drawloom technology behind their production — became popular as the aesthetics of silk were translated to other media. James Trilling linked the appearance of repeating roundels with animals across material to silk technology, in what he described as the "medallion style" of early Byzantine aesthetics (Trilling 1985). In the early Islamic period, the replication of silk patterns and motifs in woolen tapestry-weave fabrics attests to the high value medieval viewers placed on the visual effects of silk aesthetics (Dospĕl Williams 2019).

Textiles were a central aspect of the premodern aesthetic experience, not only through clothing but also through their presence in interior and exterior spaces. Tents were part of celebrations in royal gardens, and part of the spatial setting as much as permanent architecture, despite their ephemerality (Atasoy 2000; Dimmig 2016). Textiles were not only used as furnishing textiles in the built environment, but their designs and ornamental patterns moved in and out of architectural decoration, capturing ephemeral experience of fabric in more permanent form and recording a transmedial appreciation of textile aesthetics. The wall paintings of the sixth-century Red Monastery in Egypt, for example, portray curtains and textile motifs (Bolman 2016: 119–128). In Constantinople, palmettes and repeating patterns from imported Central Asian silks appear in stone in the architectural decoration of the sixth-century Church of Hagios Polyeuktos (Canepa 2010: 188–223). Such patterns were also used in textiles produced as far west as Spain and there, too, textile patterns were used in architectural decoration in a range of different media. They appear in stone on the facade of the church at Quintanilla de las Viñas (late seventh–early eighth centuries) near Silos; carved in stone both on the facade and in the interior of Santa María del Naranco (c. 842–50) near Oviedo; and in stucco carvings added to a cloister at the monastery of Santa María la Real de las Huelgas in Burgos in the late thirteenth century (Blessing 2019). Textile patterns also

Figure 66 Old trees, level distance, Guo Xi (Chinese, ca. 1000–ca. 1090), Northern Song dynasty (960–1127), ca. 1080, China. Medium: Handscroll; ink and color on silk. Dimensions: Image – 35.6 × 104.4 cm (14 × 41 1/8 in.), overall with mounting: 37.5 × 853.8 cm (14 3/4 in. × 28 ft. 1/8 in.). Metropolitan Museum of Art, New York, Gift of John M. Crawford Jr., in honor of Douglas Dillon, 1981, accession number: 1981.276. Open access CC0.

frequently appear in wall paintings in churches across present-day Spain, with significant Romanesque examples in Catalonia (Guardia 2011; Yarza Luaces 1999).

The use of textile motifs, as well as pieces of textiles extends into scroll and album leaf production in East Asia and book production in the medieval Islamic world and Europe. East Asian hand and hanging scrolls feature text or image painted (or written, with a brush) on plain-weave silk or paper, and mounted on different types of silks, often compound weaves with floral or animal patterns (Figure 66). Paintings and poetry could also be mounted on silk in an album leaf format (Figure 67). In addition to paintings and poetry, Buddhist scriptures, or sutras, were also preserved in scroll format (written by hand or printed)

Figure 67 Garden of the inept administrator, Wen Zhengming (Chinese, 1470–1559), Ming dynasty (1368–1644), 1551, China. Medium: Album of eight leaves; ink on paper. Dimensions: Image – 26.4 × 27.3 cm (10 3/8 × 10 3/4 in.), image with mounting: 39.1 × 42.5 cm (15 3/8 × 16 3/4 in.), double leaf unfolded: 39.1 × 85.1 cm (15 3/8 × 33 1/2 in.), mat: 46.5 × 86.4 cm (18 5/16 × 34 in.). Metropolitan Museum of Art, New York, Gift of Douglas Dillon, 1979, accession number: 1979.458.1a–ii. Open Access CC0.

Figure 68 Sutra cover, Ming dynasty (1368–1644), sixteenth-century China.
Medium/technique: Plain-weave silk with supplementary weft patterning.
Dimensions: Overall – 34.6 × 12.2 × 0.3 cm (13 5/8 × 4 13/16 × 1/8 in.).
Metropolitan Museum of Art, New York, purchase, Friends of Asian Art Gifts, in
honor of James C. Y. Watt, 2011, accession number: 2011.221.36. Open access CC0.

although these were usually mounted on paper. Precious religious and secular scrolls were stored in cloth bags, or covers (Figure 68), which have been collected by museums and become objects of interest in and of themselves (Gasparini 2013). In the Islamic and European contexts, textiles were included as the inner linings of book bindings, called doublures (Ohta 2021; Winter 2018), but also in other parts of bindings (Sciacca 2007). Furthermore, evidence of needle holes in Byzantine and western European manuscripts suggest that bits of textiles were also sown into books, for instance to serve as page markers or as curtains over images (Sciacca 2007). Such textiles could be both locally produced and imported since they were fragments of larger pieces used for different purposes such as dress. In Mamluk Egypt in the fifteenth century, similar motifs were used on textile and leather doublures, and also in architectural decoration carved in stone, in another example of cross-media use, although in this case the direction of motif transfer is not as clear cure as in the case of the roundel motifs described Section 5.3, which clearly originated in textiles. The importation of Byzantine silks to what is present-day Germany had an impact on the production of Ottonian manuscripts, in which textile pages frequently appear (Bücheler 2019; Sciacca 2007; Wagner 2002) One especially striking example pointing to Ottonian appreciation for imported silks appears in the late tenth-century "Quedlinburg Gospels,"[16] which features emulations of deep purple silk textiles as background for the opening words of each Gospel's sacred text. Since both silks and illuminated manuscripts were luxury products, the shared aesthetic is best placed within the larger context of what was considered both precious and beautiful in medieval courts (Wagner 2002). Much more than decorative, these pages carried specific meanings that changed depending on the type of manuscript they appeared in (Bücheler 2019).

---

[16] http://ica.themorgan.org/manuscript/thumbs/131052.

Appendix: Selection of Online Databases of Textile Holdings and Research

Brooklyn Museum, www.brooklynmuseum.org/

Cleveland Museum of Art, www.clevelandart.org/art/collection/search

Cooper Hewitt, https://collection.cooperhewitt.org/

Dumbarton Oaks Catalogue of Textiles in the Byzantine Collection, www.doaks.org/resources/textiles

Field Museum of Natural History, Chicago, https://collections-anthropology.fieldmuseum.org/

The George Washington Museum/The Textile Museum, https://collections-gwu.zetcom.net/en/

Louvre, https://collections.louvre.fr/en/

Metropolitan Museum of Art, www.metmuseum.org/art/the-collection

Textiles from the Nile Valley Research Group, www.headquarters-katoennatie.com/en/textiles-from-the-nile-valley

Textile-Dates, Abteilung Christliche Archäologie, Rheinische Friederich-Wilhelms-Universität Bonn, www.textile-dates.uni-bonn.de/

Staatliche Museen zu Berlin, https://sammlung.smb.museum/

Victoria and Albert Museum, www.vam.ac.uk/collections

Bibliography

Primary Sources

al-Din, R. (1998–99). *Jami'u't-tawarikh: Compendium of Chronicles – A History of the Mongols*, vol. 1–3. English translation and annotation by W. M. Thackston. Sources of Oriental Languages and Literatures 45, ed. Şinasi Tekin and Gönül Alpay Tekin, Central Asian Sources IV. Cambridge, MA: Harvard University Department of Near Eastern Languages and Civilizations.

al-Washsha, trans. S. Bouhlal (2004). *Le livre du brocart (al-Kitâb al-Muwashshâ) par al-Washshâ', ou La société raffinée de Bagdad au Xe siècle*. Paris: Gallimard.

Bauer, A. and Rau, R. ed. (1971). *Quellen zur Geschichte der sächsischen Kaiserzeit: Widukinds Sachsengeschichte, Adalberts Fortsetzung der Chronik Reginos, Liudprands Werke*. Darmstadt: Wissenschaftliche Buchgesellschaft.

Chen, G. F. Zhang, X. Liu, B. Dang, eds. (2011). *Yuan dian zhang*, vol. 4. Tianjin: Zhonghua shuju.

Davis, R. (2007). *The Lives of the Eighth-Century Popes (liber Pontificalis): The Ancient Biographies of Nine Popes from AD 715 to AD 817*. 2nd ed. Liverpool: Liverpool University Press.

Ghabin, A. (2009). *Hisba: Arts and Craft in Islam*. Wiesbaden: Harrassowitz Verlag.

Huang, S. (1986). *Tongzhi Tiaoge*. Hangzhou: Zhejian guji chuban she.

Koder, J. trans. (1991). *Das Eparchenbuch Leons des Weisen*. Vienna: Verlag der Österreichischen Akademie der Wissenschaften.

Legge, J. trans. (1967). *Li Chi: Book of Rites: An Encyclopedia of Ancient Ceremonial Usages, Religious Creeds, and Social Institutions* vol. 2, edited with introduction and study guide by Ch'u Chai and Winberg Chai. New Hyde Park: University Books.

Li, R. trans. (1996). *Xuanzang and Bianji, The Great Tang Dynasty Record of the Western Regions*. Berkeley, CA: Numata Center for Buddhist Translation & Research.

Mayr-Harting, H. (2001). Liudprand of Cremona's Account of his Legation to Constantinople (968) and Ottonian Imperial Strategy. *English Historical Review*, **116**(467), 539–556. https://doi-org/10.1093/enghis/116.467.539

Polo, M. (1958). *The Travels*. Trans. Ronald Latham. London: Penguin Books.

Polo, M. (1976). *The Description of the World*, Trans. Paul Pelliot and A.C. Moule. New York: AMS Press.

Procopius, trans. H. B. Dewing (1928). *History of the Wars, Volume V. Books 7.36–38. (Gothic War)*. Loeb Classical Library 217. https://doi-org/10.4159/DLCL.procopius-history_wars.1914.

Song Lian 宋濂 (1976 [1370]). *Yuan shi*. Beijing: Zhonghua shuju.

Tuotuo脱脱 (1971). *Jin shi* 金史. Taipei: Chengwen chuban she.

Tuotuo 脱脱 (1974). *Liao shi* 遼史. Beijing: Zhonghua shuju.

Tuotuo 脱脱 (1977). *Song shi* 宋史. Beijing: Zhonghua shuju.

Secondary Literature

Alchermes, J. D. (2009). *Αναθέματα εορτικά: Studies in Honor of Thomas F. Mathews*. Mainz: Philipp von Zabern.

Ansari, S., ed. (2013). Special Issue: Textile as Money on the Silk Road. *Journal of the Royal Asiatic Society*, **23**, 2.

Atasoy, N. (2000). *Otağ-ı Hümayun: Osmanlı Çadırları*. Istanbul: Aygaz.

Baker, P. L. (1995). *Islamic Textiles*. London: British Museum.

Balfour-Paul, J. (1997). *Indigo in the Arab World*. Surrey: Curzon.

Ball, J. (2005). *Byzantine Dress: Representations of Secular Dress in Eighth- to Twelfth-Century Painting*. New York: Palgrave.

Ball, J. and E. Dospel Williams (2022). "Byzantine Dress and Fashion," Byzantium and Friends podcast, January 6, 2022, www.podbean.com/ew/pb-8qxyj-1170892.

Barnes, R. (1997). *Indian Block-Printed Textiles in Egypt: The Newberry Collection in the Ashmolean Museum, Oxford*. Oxford: Ashmolean Museum, http://jameelcentre.ashmolean.org/collection/7/10236/10316.

Bénazeth, D., and P. Dal-Prà (1995). Renaissance d'une tapisserie antique. *La Revue du Louvre et des musées de France*, **4**, 29–40.

Blessing, P. (2022). Fiber Fragments: The Divided Histories of Medieval Islamic Textiles. In S. Bowker, X. Gazi, and O. Öztürk, eds., *Deconstructing the Myths of Islamic Art*. New York: Routledge, pp. 77–90.

Blessing, P. (2019). Weaving on the Wall: Architecture and Textiles in the Monastery of Las Huelgas in Burgos. *Studies in Iconography*, **40**, 137–182.

Blessing, P. (2018). Draping, Wrapping, Hanging: Transposing Textile Materiality in the Middle Age. *The Textile Museum Journal*, **45**, 2–18. https://doi-org/10.7560/TMJ4502.

Bogdanović, J. (2014). The Moveable Canopy. The Performative Space of the Major Sakkos of Metropolitan Photios. *Byzantinoslavica*, **LXXII**, 247–288.

Bogensperger, I. (2016). How to Order a Textile in Ancient Times: The Step before Distribution and Trade. In K. Dross-Krüpe and M.-L. Nosch eds. *Textiles, Trade, and Theories. From the Ancient Near East to the Mediterranean*. Münster: Ugarit-Verlag, pp. 259–280.

Bolman, E., ed. (2016). *The Red Monastery Church: Beauty and Asceticism in Upper Egypt*. New Haven: Yale University Press.

Borkopp-Restle, B. (2019). *Der Schatz der Marienkirche zu Danzig: liturgische Gewänder und textile Objekte aus dem späten Mittelalter.* Affalterbach: Didymos-Verlag.

Brubaker, L. (2004). The Elephant and the Ark: Cultural and Material Interchange across the Mediterranean in the Eighth and Ninth Centuries. *Dumbarton Oaks Papers,* **58,** 175–195, www.jstor.org/stable/3591385.

Bücheler, A. (2019). *Ornament as Argument: Textile Pages and Textile Metaphors in Early Medieval Manuscripts.* Berlin: De Gruyter.

Bühl, G. and E. Dospěl Williams (2019). *Catalogue of the Textiles in the Dumbarton Oaks Byzantine Collection.* Washington, DC: Dumbarton Oaks, www.doaks.org/resources/textiles/.

Bühl, G., S. Krody, and E. Dospěl Williams (2019). *Woven Interiors: Furnishing Early Medieval Egypt.* Washington, DC: The Textile Museum, https://museum2.drupal.gwu.edu/sites/g/files/zaxdzs3226/f/Woven%20Interiors%20Catalogue.pdf.

Burnham, D. (1980). *Warp and Weft: A Textile Terminology.* Toronto: Royal Ontario Museum.

Burns, J. (2014). *Sea of Silk: A Textile Geography of Women's Work in Medieval French Literature.* Philadelphia: University of Pennsylvania Press.

Bush, O. (2018). *Reframing the Alhambra.* Edinburgh: Edinburgh University Press.

Cabrera Lafuente, A. (2020). Textiles from the Museum of San Isidoro (Leon): New Evidence for Re-evaluating their Chronology and Provenance. In T. Martin, ed., *The Medieval Iberian Treasury in the Context of Cultural Interchange (Expanded Edition).* Leiden: Brill, pp. 81–117, https://brill.com/view/title/57009?rskey=17nl7N&result=1.

Calament, F. (2005). *La révélation d'Antinoé par Albert Gayet: Histoire, archéologie, muséographie.* Cairo: Institut français d'archéologie orientale.

Calament, F. and M. Durand, eds. (2013). *Antinoé, à la vie, à la mode. Visions d'élégance dans les solitudes.* Exhibition catalogue, Lyon: Musée des Tissus/ Fage.

Canepa, M. P. (2014). Textiles and Elite Tastes between the Mediterranean, Iran and Asia at the End of Antiquity. In M.-L. Nosch, Z. Feng and L. Varadarajan, eds., *Global Textile Encounters.* Oxford: Oxbow Books, pp. 1–14.

Canepa, M. P. (2010). *The Two Eyes of the Earth: Art and Ritual of Kingship between Rome and Sasanian Iran.* Berkeley: University of California Press.

Cardon, D. (2007). *Natural Dyes: Sources, Tradition, Technology and Science.* London: Archetype.

Carroll, D. (1998). *Looms and Textiles of the Copts, First Millennium Egyptian Textiles in the Carl Austin Rietz Collection of the California Academy of Science.* Seattle: University of Washington Press.

Caseau, B. (2007). Objects in Churches: The Testimony of Inventories. In L. Lavan, E. Swift, and T. Putzeys, eds. *Objects in Context, Objects in Use: Material Spatiality in Late Antiquity.* Leiden: Brill, pp. 551–579.

Chen, B. (2019). *Silk and Fashion in Tang China.* Seattle: University of Washington Press.

Chen, B. (2016). Material Girls: Silk and Self-Fashioning in Tang China. *Fashion Theory,* **21**(1), 5–33.

Chowdhury, Z. (2015). An Imperial Mughal Tent and Mobile Sovereignty in Eighteenth-Century Jodhpur. *Art History,* **38**(4), 668–681.

CIETA (Centre International d'Etude des Textiles Anciens) (2006). *Vocabulary of Textile Terms.* Lyon: Publications du CIETA. https://cieta.fr/cieta-vocabulaire/.

Çızakça, M. (1980). A Short History of the Bursa Silk Industry (1500-1900). *Journal of the Social and Economic History of the Orient,* **23**, 142–152.

Clark, H. (1995). Muslims and Hindus in the Culture and Morphology of Quanzhou from the Tenth to the Thirteenth Century. *Journal of World History,* **6**(1), 49–74.

Colburn, K. (2019). Loops, Tabs, and Reinforced Edges: Evidence for Textiles as Architectural Elements. In G. Bühl and E. Dospěl Williams, eds., *Catalogue of the Textiles in the Dumbarton Oaks Byzantine Collection,* ed. Washington, DC: Dumbarton Oaks, www.doaks.org/resources/textiles/essays/colburn.

Colburn, K. (2016). A Closer Look at Textiles from the Collection of the Metropolitan Museum of Art: Materials and Techniques. In: T. K. Thomas, ed., *Designing Identity: The Power of Textiles in Late Antiquity.* Exhibition Catalogue, Institute for the Study of the Ancient World, New York: Princeton University Press, pp. 126–141.

Colburn, K. (2012). Materials and Techniques of Late Antique and Early Islamic Textiles Found in Egypt. In H. C. Evans and B. Ratliff, eds., *Byzantium and Islam: Age of Transition, 7th–9th Century.* New York: Metropolitan Museum of Art, pp. 161–163.

Como, M. (2005) . Silkworms and Consorts in Nara Japan. *Asian Folklore Studies,* **64**(1), 111–131.

Compareti, M. (2003). The Role of the Sogdian Colonies in the Diffusion of the Pearl Roundels Pattern. In M. Compareti, P. Raffetta, and G. Scarcia, eds., *Ērān ud Anērān: Studies Presented to Boris Ilich Marshak on the Occasion of His 70th Birthday.* Electronic Version (October 2003) – Updated August 2006, www .transoxiana.org/Eran/Articles/compareti.html.

Contadini, A. (2013). Sharing a Taste? Material Culture and Intellectual Curiosity around the Mediterranean, from the Eleventh to the Sixteenth Century. In A. Contadini and C. Norton, eds., *The Renaissance and the Ottoman World.* Farnham and Burlington, VT: Ashgate, 2013, pp. 23–61.

De Moor, A., C. Fluck, and P. Linscheid, eds. (2015). *Drawing the Threads Together: Textiles and Footwear of the 1st Millennium AD from Egypt; Proceedings of the 7th Conference of the Research Group "Textiles from the Nile Valley," Antwerp, 7–9 October 2011.* Tielt: Lannoo.

Denney, J. (2016). Elite Mongol Dress of the Yuan Dynasty (1271-1368): Focusing on Textiles Woven with Gold. In J. von Fircks and R. Schorta, eds., *Oriental Silks in Medieval Europe.* Riggisberger Berichte 21. Riggisberg: Abegg-Stiftung, pp. 124–135.

Denny, W. B. and S. B. Krody (2002). *The Classical Tradition in Anatolian Carpets.* Washington, DC: Textile Museum.

Dimmig, A. (2016). Fabricating a New Image: Imperial Tents in the Late Ottoman Period. In C. J. Gruber, ed., *Islamic Architecture on the Move: Motion and Modernity,* Bristol: Intellect, pp. 103–133.

Dodds J. D. ed. (1992). *Al-Andalus: The Art of Islamic Spain.* New York: Metropolitan Museum of Art.

Dolezalek, I. (2013). Textile Connections? Two Ifrīqiyan Church Treasuries in Norman Sicily and the Problem of Continuity across Political Change. *al-Masāq: Journal of the Medieval Mediterranean,* **25**(1), 92–112. https://doi .org/10.1080/09503110.2013.767009.

Donkin, R. (1977). The Insect Dyes of Western and West-Central Asia. *Anthropos,* **72**(5/6), 847–80.

Dospěl Williams, E. (2023). The Mobility of Fabric: Textiles in and around Medieval Eurasia. In A. Luyster, ed., *Bringing the Holy Land Home The Crusades, Chertsey Abbey, and the Reconstruction of a Medieval Masterpiece.* London: Harvey Miller, pp. 177–200.

Dospěl Williams, E. (2022). Adoption, Adaptation, Reinterpretation: Inscribed Textiles in Medieval Egypt's Christian and Jewish Communities. In M. McWilliams and J. Sokoly, eds., *Social Fabrics.* Cambridge MA: Harvard University Art Museums, pp. 31–38.

Dospěl Williams, E. (2019). A Taste for Textiles: Designing Umayyad and Early ʿAbbāsid Interiors. *Dumbarton Oaks Papers,* **73**, 409–432, www.jstor.org/ stable/26955185.

Dospěl Williams, E. (2018a). Appealing to the Senses: Experiencing Adornment in the Early Medieval Eastern Mediterranean. In F. Griffiths and K. Starkey, eds., *Sensory Reflections: Traces of Experience in Medieval Artifacts.* Berlin: De Gruyter, pp. 78–96.

Dospěl Williams, E. (2018b). Gems in Cloth and Stone: Medium, Materiality, and the Late Antique Jeweled Aesthetic. *The Textile Museum Journal,* **45**, 22–39, https://doi.org/10.7560/TMJ4503.

Dusenbury, M. M. (2015). Color at the Court of Japan in the Heian Period. In Mary M. Dusenbury (ed.), *Color in Ancient and Medieval East Asia*. Lawrence: Spencer Museum of Art, University of Kansas, New Haven: Yale University Press, pp. 163–177.

Eastmond, A. and L. Jones (2001). Robing, Power, and Legitimacy in Armenia and Georgia. In S. Gordon, ed., *Robes and Honor: The Medieval World of Investiture*. New York: Palgrave, pp. 241–254.

Ekici, D., B. Baudez, and P. Blessing, ed. (2023). *Textile in Architecture: From the Middle Ages to Modernity*. New York: Routledge.

Eldem, E. (2016). The Genesis of the Museum of Turkish and Islamic Arts. In M. Farhad and S. Rettig, eds., *The Art of the Qur'an: Treasures from the Museum of Turkish and Islamic Arts* Washington, DC: Arthur M. Sackler Gallery, Smithsonian Institution, pp. 118–139.

El Rashidi, S. and S. Bowker (2018). *The Tentmakers of Cairo: Egypt's Medieval and Modern Applique Craft*. Cairo: The American University in Cairo Press.

El-Sayed, R. and C. Fluck (2020). *The Textile Centre Akhmîm-Panopolis (Egypt) in Late Antiquity: Material Evidence for Continuity and Change in Society, Religion, Industry and Trade: Proceedings of the International Conference Organised by Georg-August-Universität Göttingen in Cooperation with Skulpturensammlung und Museum für Byzantinische Kunst der Staatlichen Museen zu Berlin – Preußischer Kulturbesitz, Göttingen, 28-30 September 2017*. Wiesbaden: Reichert Verlag.

Elsberg, H. A. and R. Guest (1934). Another Silk Fabric Woven in Baghdad. *The Burlington Magazine for Connoisseurs*, **64**(375), 270–272, www.jstor.org/stable/865888.

Emery, I. (2009). *The Primary Structures of Fabrics: An Illustrated Classification*. London and Washington, DC: Thames and Hudson and The Textile Museum.

Emon, A. M. (2012). *Religious Pluralism in Islamic Law: Dhimmis and Others in the Empire of Law*. Oxford: Oxford University Press.

Ertuğ, A. (1996). *Silks for the Sultans: Ottoman Imperial garments from Topkapi Palace*. Istanbul: Ertuğ & Kocabıyık.

Evans, H. C. and B. Ratliff, eds. (2012). *Byzantium and Islam: Age of Transition, 7th–9th Century*. New York: Metropolitan Museum of Art.

Featherstone, J. M. (2005). The Chrysotriklinos Seen through De Cerimoniis. In L. M. Hoffmann, ed., *Zwischen Polis, Provinz und Peripherie: Beiträge zur byzantinischen Geschichte und Kultur*. Wiesbaden: Harrassowitz, pp. 845–852.

Fehlmann, M., M. Matzke, and S. Söll-Tauchert (2019). *Gold & Ruhm: Kunst und Macht unter Kaiser Heinrich II*. Basel: Historisches Museum Basel and Munich: Hirmer.

Feliciano, M. J. (2020). Sovereign, Saint, and City: Honor and Reuse of Textiles in the Treasury of San Isidoro (Leon). In T. Martin, ed., *The Medieval Iberian Treasury in the Context of Cultural Interchange (Expanded Edition)*. Leiden: Brill, pp. 118–144. Open access online edition: https://brill.com/view/title/57009?rskey=17nl7N&result=1.

Feliciano, M. J. (2014). Medieval Textiles in Iberia: Studies for a New Approach. In D. J. Roxburgh, ed., *Envisioning Islamic Art and Architecture: Essays in Honor of Renata Holod*. Leiden: Brill, pp. 46–65.

Feliciano, M. J. (2005). Muslim Shrouds for Christian Kings? A Reassessment of Andalusi Textiles in Thirteenth-Century Castilian Life and Ritual. In C. Robinson and L. Rouhi, eds., *Under the Influence: Questioning the Comparative in Medieval Castile*. Leiden: Brill, pp. 101–132.

Fluck, C. and G. Helmecke, ed. (2006). *Textile Messages: Inscribed Fabrics from Roman to Abbasid Egypt*. Leiden: Brill.

Fulghum, M. M. (2001–02). Under Wraps: Byzantine Textiles as Major and Minor Arts. *Studies in the Decorative Arts*, **9**(1), 13–33, www.jstor.org/stable/40662797.

Gajewski, A. and S. Seeberg (2016). Having Her Hand In It? Elite Women as 'Makers' of Textile Art in the Middle Ages. *Journal of Medieval History*, **42**(1), 26–50, https://doi.org/10.1080/03044181.2015.1106970.

Galliker, J. (2017). Terminology Associated with Silk in the Middle Byzantine Period (AD 843-1204). In S. Gaspa, C. Michel, and M.-L. Nosch, eds., *Textile Terminologies from the Orient to the Mediterranean and Europe, 1000 BC to 1000 AD*. Lincoln, NE: Zea Books, pp. 346–373, https://halshs.archives-ouvertes.fr/halshs-01674057.

Galliker, J. (2015a). Middle Byzantine Silk in Context: Integrating the Textual and Material Evidence. Ph.D thesis, University of Birmingham.

Galliker, J. (2015b). Application of Computer Vision to Analysis of Historic Silk Textiles. In A. De Moor, C. Fluck, and P. Linscheid, eds., *Drawing the Threads Together: Textiles and Footwear of the 1st Millennium AD from Egypt; Proceedings of the 7th Conference of the Research Group "Textiles from the Nile Valley," Antwerp, 7–9 October 2011*. Tielt: Lannoo, pp. 150–163.

Garrison, E. (2017). Mimetic Bodies: Repetition, Replication, and Simulation in the Marriage Charter of Empress Theophanu, *Word & Image*, **33**(2), 212–232.

Garver, V. L. (2018). Sensory Experiences of Low-Status Female Textile Workers in the Carolingian World. In F. Griffiths and K. Starkey, eds., *Sensory Reflections: Traces of Experience in Medieval Artifacts*. Berlin: De Gruyter, 50–76.

Gasparini, M. (2019). *Transcending Patterns: Silk Road Cultural and Artistic Interactions through Central Asian Textiles*. Honolulu: University of Hawai'i Press.

Gasparini, M. (2013). The Silk Cover of the *Admonitions* Scroll: Aesthetic and Visual Analysis. In Paolo Santangelo ed., *Ming Qing Studies*. Rome: Aracne editrice, pp. 161–218.

Goitein, S. D. (1983). *A Mediterranean Society: The Jewish Communities of the Arab World as Portrayed in the Documents of the Cairo Geniza*, vol. 4. *Daily Life*. Berkeley: University of California Press.

Goitein, S. D. (1973). *Letters of Medieval Jewish Traders*. Princeton University Press.

Goitein, S. D. (1967). *A Mediterranean Society: The Jewish Communities of the Arab World as Portrayed in the Cairo Geniza*, vol. 1. Berkeley: University of California Press.

Goitein, S. D. and M. Friedman (2007). *Indian Traders of the Middle Ages: Documents from the Cairo Geniza*. Leiden: Brill.

Gordon, S. D., ed. (2001). *Robes and Honor: The Medieval World of Investiture*. New York: Palgrave.

Grabar, O. and S. Blair (1980). *Epic Images and Contemporary History: The Illustrations of the Great Mongol Shahnama*. Chicago, IL: University of Chicago Press.

Guardia, M. (2011). *San Baudelio de Berlanga: Una encrucijada*. Barcelona: Universitat Autònoma de Barcelona.

Hambly, G. R. G. (2001). From Baghdad to Bukhara, from Ghazna to Delhi: The Khil'a Ceremony in the Transmission of Kingly Pomp and Circumstance. In S. Gordon, ed., *Robes and Honor: The Medieval World of Investiture*. New York: Palgrave, pp. 193–222.

Hansen, V. (2016). *Silk Road: A New History with Documents*. Oxford: Oxford University Press.

Harris, S. (2019). The Sensory Archaeology of Textiles. In R. Skeates and J. Day, ed., *The Routledge Handbook of Sensory Archaeology*. New York: Routledge, pp. 210–232.

Hillenbrand, R. (2011). Propaganda in the Mongol "World History". *British Academy Review*, **17**, 29–38.

Hoffman, E. R. (2001). Pathways of Portability: Islamic and Christian Interchange from the Tenth to the Twelfth Century. *Art History*, **24**, 17–50.

Hoffman, E. R. and S. Redford (2017). Transculturation in the Eastern Mediterranean. In F. B. Flood and G. Necipoğlu, eds., *A Companion to Islamic Art and Architecture*. Hoboken, NJ: John Wiley & Sons, vol. 1, pp. 405–430.

Hoskins, N. A. (2004). *The Coptic Tapestry Albums and the Archaeologist of Antinoé, Albert Gayet*. Seattle: University of Washington Press.

Houghteling, S. (2020). Dyeing the Springtime: The Art and Poetry of Fleeting Textile Colors in Medieval and Early Modern South Asia. *Religions*, **11**(12), 627–646. https://doi.org/10.3390/rel11120627.

Hu, J. (2017). Global Medieval at the End of the Silk Road circa 756 CE: The Shōsō-in Collection in Japan. *The Medieval Globe*, **3**(2), 177–202.

Jackson, P. (2017). *The Mongols and the Islamic World*. New Haven: Yale University Press.

Jacoby, D. (2017). The Production and Diffusion of Andalusi Silk and Silk Textiles, Mid-Eighth to Mid-Thirteenth Century. In A. Shalem, ed., *The Chasuble of Thomas Becket*. Munich: Hirmer Verlag, pp. 142–151.

Jacoby, D. (2016). Oriental Silks at the Time of the Mongols: Patterns of Trade and Distribution in the West. *Oriental Silks in Medieval Europe. Riggisberger Berichte*, **21**, 92–123.

Jacoby, D. (2008). Silk Production. In E. Jeffreys, J. Haldon and R. Cormack, eds., *The Oxford Handbook of Byzantine Studies*. Oxford: Oxford University Press, pp. 421–428.

Jacoby, D. (2004). Silk Economics and Cross-Cultural Artistic Interaction: Byzantium, the Muslim World, and the Christian West. *Dumbarton Oaks Papers*, **58**, 197–240. www.jstor.org/stable/3591386.

Jacoby, D. (1991–92). Silk in Western Byzantium before the Fourth Crusade. *Byzantinische Zeitschrift*, **84/85**, 470–488.

Jeroussalimskaja, A. (1993). Soieries sassanides. In *Splendeur des Sassanides: L'empire perse entre Rome et la Chine*. Brussels: Musees royaux d'Art et d'Histoire, pp. 113–120.

Kadoi, Y. (2009). *Islamic Chinoiserie: The Art of Mongol Iran*. Edinburgh: Edinburgh University Press.

Kelley, A. (2022). Searching for Professional Women in the Mid- to Late-Roman Textile Industry. *Past & Present*, **258**(1), 3–43. https://academic.oup.com/past/article/258/1/3/6652269.

Kelley, A. (2019). By Land or by Sea: Tracing the Adoption of Cotton in the Economies of the Mediterranean. In M. Ivanova and H. Jeffries, eds., *Transmitting and Circulating the Late Antique and Byzantine Worlds*. Leiden: Brill, pp. 274–297.

Kinoshita, S. (2004). Almería and the French Feudal Imaginary: Toward a "Material" History of the Medieval Mediterranean. In J. Burns, ed., *Medieval Fabrications: Dress, Textiles, Clothwork, and Other Cultural Imaginings*. New York: Palgrave Macmillan, pp. 165–176.

Kirby, J. (2014), *Natural Colourants for Dyeing and Lake Pigments: Practical Recipes and their Historical Sources*. London: Archetype.

Krody, S. (2019). Comfort at Home. In G. Bühl, S. Krody, and E. Dospěl Williams, eds., *Woven Interiors: Furnishing Early Medieval Egypt*. Washington, DC: The Textile Museum, pp. 80–87, https://museum2.drupal .gwu.edu/sites/g/files/zaxdzs3226/f/Woven%20Interiors%20Catalogue.pdf.

Kuhn, D. (1984). Tracing a Chinese Legend: In Search of the Identity of the "First Sericulturalist." *T'oung Pao*, **70**, 213–245.

Kuhn, D. and Zhao F., eds. (2012). *Chinese Silks*. New Haven: Yale University Press.

Kwaspen, A. and C. Verhecken-Lammens (2015). Measurements and Fitting of Egyptian Children's Tunics of the 1st Millennium AD. In A. De Moor, C. Fluck, and P. Linscheid, eds., *Textiles, Tools and Techniques: Proceedings of the 8th Conference of the Research Group 'Textiles from the Nile Valley,"* 4-6 October 2013. Tielt: Lannoo, pp. 152–167.

Lamm, C. (1937). *Cotton in Mediaeval Textiles of the Near East*. Paris: P. Geuthner.

Levy-Rubin, M. (2011). *Non-Muslims in the Early Islamic Empire: From Surrender to Coexistence*. Cambridge: Cambridge University Press.

Lingley, K. A. (2010). Naturalizing the Exotic: On the Changing Meanings of Ethnic Dress in Medieval China. *Ars Orientalis*, **38**, 50–80.

Liu, X. (2010). *The Silk Road in World History*. Oxford: Oxford University Press.

Lo, J. (2012). *China as a Sea Power, 1127–1368: A Preliminary Survey of the Maritime Expansion and Naval Exploits of the Chinese People during the Southern Song and Yuan Periods*. Singapore: NUS Press.

Lopez, R. S. (1945). Silk Industry in the Byzantine Empire. *Speculum*, **20**(1), 1–42. www.jstor.org/stable/2851187.

Luyster, A. (2021). Reassembling Textile Networks: Treasuries and Re-Collecting Practices in Thirteenth-Century England. *Speculum*, **96**(4), 1039–1078.

Mack, R. (2001). *Bazaar to Piazza: Islamic Trade and Italian Art, 1300-1600*. Berkeley: University of California Press.

Mackie, L. W. (2015). *Symbols of Power: Luxury Textiles from Islamic Lands, 7th-21st Century*. Cleveland: Cleveland Museum of Art and Yale University Press.

Mackie, L. W. (1984). Toward an Understanding of Mamluk Silks: National and International Considerations. *Muqarnas*, **2**, 127–146.

Maguire, E. D. (2019). Curtains at the Threshold: How They Hung and How They Performed. In G. Bühl and E. Dospěl Williams, eds., *Catalogue of the*

Textiles in the Dumbarton Oaks Byzantine Collection. Washington, DC: Dumbarton Oaks, www.doaks.org/resources/textiles/essays/maguire.

Maniatis, G (1999). Organization, Market Structure, and Modus Operandi of the Private Silk Industry in Tenth-Century Byzantium. *Dumbarton Oaks Papers*, **53**, 236–332. www.jstor.org/stable/1291804.

Martin, T., ed. (2020). *The Medieval Iberian Treasury in the Context of Cultural Interchange (Expanded Edition)*. Leiden: Brill, https://brill.com/view/title/57009?rskey=17nl7N&result=1.

Martiniani-Reber, M. (1999). Tentures et textiles des églises romaines au haut Moyen Âge d'après le *Liber pontificalis*. *Mélanges de l'école française de Rome*, **111**(1), 289–305.

McWilliams, M. and J. Sokoly, eds. (2022). *Social Fabrics: Inscribed Textiles from Medieval Egyptian Tombs*. Cambridge, MA: Harvard Art Museums.

Metcalfe, A. and M. Rosser-Owen. (2013). Forgotten Connections? Medieval Material Culture and Exchange in the Central and Western Mediterranean. *al-Masāq: Journal of the Medieval Mediterranean*, **25**(1), 1–8. https://doi.org/10.1080/09503110.2013.767010.

Monnas, L. (2010). The Impact of Oriental Silks on Italian Silk Weaving in the Fourteenth Century. In L. E. Saurma-Jeltsch and A. Eisenbeiß, eds., *The Power of Things and the Flow of Cultural Transformations*. Berlin and Munich: Deutscher Kunstverlag, pp. 65–83.

Monnas, L. (2008). *Merchants, Princes, and Painters: Silk Fabrics in Italian and Northern Paintings 1300-1500*. New Haven: Yale University Press.

Mühlemann, C. (2022). Made in Baghdad? Medieval Textile Production and Pattern Notation Systems of Early Woven Lampas Silks. *Muqarnas*, **39**, 1–21.

Mühlemann, C. (2017). Inscribed Horizontal Bands on Two Cloth-of-Gold Panels and Their Function as Part of an Īlkḫānid Dress. *Ars Orientalis*, **47**, 43–68.

Munroe, N. H. (2012). Early Islamic Textiles: Inscribed Garment. The Metropolitan Museum of Art Blog, July 2, 2012, www.metmuseum.org/exhibitions/listings/2012/byzantium-and-islam/blog/topical-essays/posts/inscribed-garments.

Muthesius, A. (1997). *Byzantine Silk Weaving, AD 400 to AD 1200*. Vienna: Verlag Fassbaender.

Muthesius, A. (1995). The Impact of the Mediterranean Silk Trade on Western Europe before 1200 AD. In A. Muthesius, ed., *Studies in Byzantine and Islamic Silk Weaving*. London: The Pindar Press, pp. 135–143.

Muthesius, A. (1992). Silken Diplomacy. In J. Shepard and S. Franklin, eds., *Byzantine Diplomacy: Papers from the Twenty-fourth Spring Symposium of Byzantine Studies, Cambridge March 1990*, Aldershot: Ashgate, pp. 237–248.

Nagel, A. (2011). Twenty-Five Notes on Pseudoscript in Italian Art. *RES*, **59–60**, 229–248, www.jstor.org/stable/23647792.

Nosch, M.-L., F. Zhao, and L. Varadarajan, eds., (2014). *Global Textile Encounters*. Oxford: Oxbow Books.

Oepen, J., B. Päffgen, S. Schrenk, U. Tegtmeier, eds. (2011). *Die Textilien aus dem hölzernen Schrein in St. Severin: Der hl. Severin von Köln. Befunde der Schreinsöffnung von 1999. Studien zur Kölner Kirchengeschichte* 37. Siegburg: Schmitt.

Ohta, A. (2021). Looking Inside the Book: Doublures of the Mamluk Period. In R. Hillenbrand, ed. *The Making of Islamic Art: Studies in Honour of Sheila Blair and Jonathan Bloom*. Edinburgh: Edinburgh University Press, pp. 184–206.

Oikonomides, N. (1986). Silk Trade and Production in Byzantium from the Sixth to the Ninth Century: The Seals of Kommerkiarioi. *Dumbarton Oaks Papers*, **40**, 33–51, www.jstor.org/stable/1291528.

Otavsky, K. (1997). Remarques techniques concernant des tissus égyptiens, perses et ibériques de la Fondation Abegg. In M. ʿA. M. Salīm, ed., *Islamische Textilkunst des Mittelalters: Aktuelle Probleme*. Riggisberg: Abegg-Stiftung, pp. 147–156.

Parani, M. G. (2019). Curtains in the Middle and Late Byzantine House. *Dumbarton Oaks Papers*, In G. Bühl and E. Dospěl Williams, eds. *Catalogue of the Textiles in the Dumbarton Oaks Byzantine Collection*. Washington, DC: Dumbarton Oaks, https://www.doaks.org/resources/textiles/essays/parani.

Partearroyo, C. (1992). Almoravid and Almohad Textiles. In J. D. Dodds, ed., *Al-Andalus: The Art of Islamic Spain*. New York: Metropolitan Museum of Art, pp. 105–106.

Pentcheva, B. V. (2015). The Power of Glittering Materiality: Mirror Reflections Between Poetry and Architecture in Greek and Arabic Medieval Culture. *Ancient Near Eastern Studies, Supplementa*, **47**, 223–268.

Phillips, A. (2021). *Sea Change: Ottoman Textiles Between the Mediterranean and the Indian Ocean*. Berkeley: University of California Press.

Phipps, E. (2011). *Looking at Textiles: A Guide to Technical Terms*. Los Angeles: The J. Paul Getty Museum.

Piltz, E. (2013). *Loros and Sakkos. Studies in Byzantine Imperial Garment and Ecclesiastical Vestment*. Oxford: Archaeopress.

Pleșa, A. D. (2017). Religious Belief in Burial: Funerary Dress and Practice at the Late Antique and Early Islamic Cemeteries at Matmar and Mostagedda, Egypt (Late Fourth–Early Ninth Centuries CE). *Ars Orientalis*, **47**, 18–42, https://quod.lib.umich.edu/a/ars/13441566.0047.002/.

Pritchard, F. (2006). *Clothing Culture: Dress in Egypt in the First Millennium AD*. Manchester: Whitworth Art Gallery.

Ptak, R. (1998). From Quanzhou to the Sulu Zone and Beyond: Questions Related to the Early Fourteenth Century. *Journal of Southeast Asian Studies*, **29**(2), 269–294.

Redford, S. (2012). Portable Palaces: On the Circulation of Objects and Ideas about Architecture in Medieval Anatolia and Mesopotamia. *Medieval Encounters*, **18**, 382–412.

Ritter, M. (2010). Kunst mit Botschaft: Der Gold-Seide-Stoff für den Ilchan Abū Saʿīd von Iran (Grabgewand Rudolfs IV. in Wien) – Rekonstruktion, Typus, Repräsentationsmedium. In M. Ritter and L. Korn, eds., *Beiträge zur Islamischen Kunst und Archäologie herausgegegeben von der Ernst-Herzfeld-Gesellschaft*. Wiesbaden: Ludwig Reichert Verlag, vol. 2, pp. 105–135.

Robinson, C. (2018). Tents of Silk and Trees of Light in the Lands of the Najd. In M. Frishkopf and F. Spinetti, ed., *Music, Sound, and Architecture in Islam*. Austin: University of Texas Press, pp. 199–122.

Rooijakkers, C. T. (2017). New Styles, New Fashions: Dress in Early Byzantine and Islamic Egypt (5th – 8th centuries). In H. Amirav and F. Celia, eds., *New Themes, New Styles in the Eastern Mediterranean: Christian, Jewish, and Islamic Encounters (5th-8th Centuries)*. Leuven: Peeters, pp. 173–203.

Rosenfeld, Y. (2016). Indian Block-Printed Textiles: Past and Present. Metropolitan Museum Blog, November 15, 2016, www.metmuseum.org/blogs/ruminations/2016/indian-block-printed-textiles.

Rosser-Owen, M. (2015). Islamic Objects in Christian Contexts: Relic Translation and Modes of Transfer in Medieval Iberia. *Art in Translation* **7**(1), 39–63, https://doi.org/10.2752/175613115X14235644692275.

Saba, M. D. (2012). Abbasid Lusterwares and the Aesthetics of ʿAjab, *Muqarnas*, **29**, 187–212.

Sanders, P. (2001). Robes of Honor in Fatimid Egypt. In S. Gordon, ed., *Robes and Honor: The Medieval World of Investiture*. New York: Palgrave, pp. 225–240.

Sanders, P. (1994). *Ritual, Politics, and the City in Fatimid Cairo*. Saratoga Springs: State University of New York Press.

Schorta, R. (2010). *Die Stoffe in den Hildesheimer Schreinen: Zu Textilien im Reliquienkult und zu Luxusgeweben im hochmittelalterlichen Europa*. Cologne: Sigurd Greven Stiftung.

Schulz, V.-S. (2018). Schriftgestöber und geritztes Gold. Orientalisierende Inschriften in der toskanischen Tafelmalerei um 1300. In W. E. Keil, S. Kiyanrad, C. Theis and L. Willer, eds., *Zeichentragende Artefakte im sakralen Raum zwischen Präsenz und UnSichtbarkeit*. Berlin: DeGruyter, pp. 215–244, https://doi.org/10.1515/9783110619928-010.

Schulz, V.-S. (2016). Crossroads of Cloth: Textile Arts and Aesthetics in and beyond the Medieval Islamic World. *Perspective: Actualité en histoire de l'art*, **1**, 93–108.

Sciacca, C. (2007). Raising the Curtain on the Use of Textiles in Manuscripts. In K. M. Rudy and B. Baert, eds., *Weaving, Veiling, and Dressing: Textiles and Their Metaphors in the Late Middle Ages*, Turnhout: Brepols, pp. 161–189.

Serjeant, R. B. (1972). *Islamic Textiles: Material for a History up to the Mongol Conquest*. Beirut: Librairie du Liban.

Shalem, A. (2019). "You Carried the Moon in the Folds of Your Sleeve": A Note on Wide-Sleeved Garments from Arabic Sources. *Zeitschrift des Deutschen Vereins für Kunstwissenschaft (Opus: Festschrift für Rainer Kahsnitz)*, **71**, 57–72.

Shalem, A., ed. (2017). *The Chasuble of Thomas Becket: A Biography*. Munich: Hirmer.

Shalem, A. (2015). The Body of Architecture: The Early History of the Clothing of the Sacred House of the Ka'ba in Mecca. In M. Kapustka and W. T. Woodfin, eds., *Clothing the Sacred: Medieval Textiles as Fabric, Form, and Metaphor*. Berlin: Edition Imorde, pp. 173–188.

Shalem, A. (2006). Manipulations of Seeing and Visual Strategies in the Audience Halls of the Early Islamic Period. In F. A. Bauer, ed., *Visualisierungen von Herrschaft: Frühmittelalterliche Residenzen; Gestalt und Zeremoniell; Internationales Kolloquium 3./4. Juni 2004 in Istanbul*. Istanbul: Ege Yayınları, pp. 213–232.

Shea, E. L. (2021a). Chinese Textiles in Mamluk Tombs: Maritime Trade and Cultural Exchange in the Fourteenth Century. In R. Dalal, S. Roberts, and J. Sokoly, eds., *The Seas and the Mobility of Islamic Art*. New Haven: Yale University Press, pp. 102–117.

Shea, E. L. (2021b). The Spread of Gold Thread in the Mongol Period. *Journal of Song Yuan Studies*, **50**, 381–415.

Shea, E. L. (2020). *Mongol Court Dress, Identity Formation, and Global Exchange*. New York: Routledge.

Shea, E. L. (2018). Painted Silks: Form and Production of Women's Court Dress in the Mongol Empire. *The Textile Museum Journal*, **45**, 36–55.

Shepherd, D. G. (1957). A Dated Hispano-Islamic Silk. *Ars Orientalis*, **2**, 373–382, www.jstor.org/stable/4629043.

Sigl, J. (2020). Egyptian Pit-looms from the Late First Millennium AD – Attempts in Reconstruction from the Archaeological Evidence. In M. Mossakowska-Gaubert, ed., *Egyptian Textiles and their Production: "Word" and "Object"*

(Hellenistic, Roman, and Byzantine Periods). Lincoln, NE: Zea Books, pp. 22–35.

Sokoly, J. A. (1997). Between Life and Death: The Funerary Context of Ṭirāz Textiles. In M. A. M. Salim, ed., *Islamische Textilkunst des Mittelalters: Aktuelle Probleme*. Riggisberg: Abegg-Stiftung, pp. 71–77.

Spuhler, F. (2014). *Pre-Islamic Carpets and Textiles from Eastern Land*s. London: Thames & Hudson.

Stauffer, A. (2008). *Antike Musterblätter: Wirkkartons aus dem spätantiken und frühbyzantinischen Ägypten*. Wiesbaden: Reichert Verlag.

Stauffer, A. (2016). *Die kostbaren Hüllen der Heiligen – Textile Schätze aus Kölner Reliquienschreinen: Neue Funde und Forschungen. Colonia Romanica: Jahrbuch des Fördervereins Romanische Kirchen Köln e.V., 31*. Cologne: Grevas.

Stephenson, J. W. (2014). Veiling the Late Roman House. *Textile History*, **45**(1), 3–31, https://doi.org/10.1179/0040496914Z.00000000035.

Stillman, Y. K. (2000). *Arab Dress. A Short History from the Dawn of Islam to Modern Times*. Leiden: Brill.

Stillman, Y. K., P. Sanders, and N. Rabbat (2012). Ṭirāz. In *Encyclopaedia of Islam*, 2nd ed., eds. P. Bearman, Th. Bianquis, C. E. Bosworth, E. van Donzel, W. P. Heinrichs. Consulted online on September 22, 2021, http://dx.doi.org.ezp-prod1.hul.harvard.edu/10.1163/1573-3912_islam_COM_1228. First published online: 2012.

Sullivan, A. (2021). Byzantine Artistic Traditions in Moldavian Church Embroideries. *Cahiers Balkaniques*, **48**, 125–162.

Susmann, N. (2020). Tyrian, True, Royal, or Real: Archaeological Assumptions about the Roman Murex Dye Industry. *Journal of Eastern Mediterranean Archaeology and Heritage Studies*, **8**(2), 159–173, www.muse.jhu.edu/article/758410.

Tezcan, H. (2006). *Osmanlı Sarayının Çocukları: Şehzadeler ve Hanım Sultanların Yaşamları, Giysileri*. Istanbul: Aygaz.

Theologou, J., A. Ozoline, and Y. Sarzetakis (2008). Fustat Carpet Fragments. *Hali*, **156**, 65–71.

Thomas, T. K. (2017). Perspectives on the Wide World of Luxury in Later Antiquity: Silk and other Exotic Textiles found in Syria and Egypt. In B. Hildebrandt and C. Gills. *Silk: Trade & Exchange along the Silk Roads between Rome and China in Antiquity*. Oxford: Oxbow Books, pp. 51–81, https://doi.org/10.2307/j.ctvh1dsv4.9.

Thomas, T. K. ed. (2016). *Designing Identity: The Power of Textiles in Late Antiquity*. Exhibition Catalogue, Institute for the Study of the Ancient World, New York. Princeton: Princeton University Press.

Thomas, T. K. (2012). Silks. In H. Evans and B. Ratliff, eds., *Byzantium and Islam: Age of Transition, 7th–9th Century*. New York: Metropolitan Museum of Art, p. 148.

Thomas, T. K. (2009). Coptic Textiles in the Dikran G. Kelekian Textile Album of c. 1910. In J. D. Alchermes, ed., *Αναθέματα εορτικά: Studies in Honor of Thomas F. Mathews*. Mainz: Philipp von Zabern, pp. 303–312.

Trilling, J. (1985). *The Medallion Style: A Study in the Origins of Byzantine Taste*. New York: Garland.

Tronzo, W. (2001). The Mantle of Roger II of Sicily. In S. Gordon, ed., *Robes and Honor: The Medieval World of Investiture*. New York: Palgrave, pp. 241–254.

Van der Vliet, J. (2006). "In a Robe of Gold": Status, Magic and Politics on Inscribed Christian Textiles from Egypt. In C. Fluck and G. Helemecke, eds., *Textile Messages: Inscribed Fabrics from Roman to Abbasid Egypt*. Leiden: Brill, pp. 23–67.

von Verschuer, C. (2008). Le costume de Heian. *Cipango: Cahier d'études japonaises, Hors-série, Autour du Genji monogatari*, Online edition February 28, 2012, accessed April 30, 2019, http://journals.openedition.org/cipango/1029 ; DOI : 10.4000/cipango.1029.

Vryzidis, N. (2020). *The Hidden Life of Textiles in the Medieval and Early Modern Mediterranean: Contexts and Cross-Cultural Encounters in the Islamic, Latinate and Eastern Christian Worlds*. Turnhout: Brepols.

Vryzidis, N. (2019a). Ottoman Textiles and Greek Clerical Vestments: Prolegomena on a Neglected Aspect of Ecclesiastical Material Culture. *Byzantine and Modern Greek Studies*, **42**(1), 92–114, https://doi.org/10.1017/byz.2017.22.

Vryzidis, N. (2019b). The "Arabic" Stole of Vatopediou Monastery: Traces of Islamic Material Culture in Late Byzantium. *Muqarnas*, **36**, 85–100.

Wagner, S. (2002). The Impact of Silk on Ottonian and Salian Manuscripts. Textile Society of America Symposium Proceedings. Textile Society of America, https://digitalcommons.unl.edu/tsaconf/554/.

Walker, A. (2012). "The Art that Does Not Think": Byzantine "Decorative Arts" – History and Limits of a Concept. *Studies in Iconography*, **34**, 169–193.

Walker, A. (2010). Patterns of Flight: Middle Byzantine Appropriation of the Chinese Feng-Huang Bird. *Ars Orientalis*, **38**, 188–216.

Wang, P. (2000). *Aching for Beauty: Footbinding in China*. Minneapolis: University of Minnesota Press.

Wardwell, A. E. (1988–89). Panni Tartarici: Eastern Islamic Silks Woven with Gold and Silver (13th and 14th centuries). *Islamic Art*, **3**, 94–147.

Wardwell, A. E. and J. C. Y. Watt (1988). *When Silk Was Gold: Central Asian and Chinese Textiles*. New York: Harry N. Abrams.

Weddigen, T. (2013). Notes from the Field: Materiality. *Art Bulletin*, **95**(1), 34–37, www.jstor.org/stable/43188793.

Wertz, J., M. Winter, R. Hanson, and M. Montague (2022). Beyond the Surface: Technical Analysis of Egyptian Textiles, c. 4th-12th Centuries. In M. McWilliams and J. Sokoly, eds., *Social Fabrics: Inscribed Textiles from Medieval Egyptian Tombs*. Cambridge, MA: Harvard Art Museums, pp. 51–61.

Wetter, E., K. Starkey, and L. Auberson, eds. (2019). *Animals in Text and Textile: Storytelling in the Medieval World*. Riggisberg: Abegg-Stiftung.

Wild, J.-P. and F. Wild (2014). Berenike and Textile Trade on the Indian Ocean. In K. Droß-Krüpe, ed., *Textile Trade and Distribution in Antiquity. Textilhandel und -distribution in der Antike*. Wiesbaden: Harrassowitz Verlag, pp. 91–109.

Willers, D. and B. Niekamp (2015). *Der Dionysosbehang der Abegg-Stiftung*. Riggisberg: Abegg-Stiftung.

Winter, M. L. (2020). When Curtains Fall: A Shape-Shifting Silk of the Late Abbasid Period. *The Medieval Globe*, **6**(1), 31–55.

Winter, M. L. (2018). Put a Bird on It: What an Aviary Preoccupation Reveals about Medieval Silks. *The Textile Museum Journal*, **45**, 61–83.

Wipszycka, E. (1965). *L'industrie textile dans l'Egypte romaine*. Wrocław: Zakład Narodowy im. Ossolińskich.

Woodfin, W. T. (2021). Textile Media. In E. Schwartz, ed., *The Oxford Handbook of Byzantine Art and Architecture*. Oxford: Oxford University Press, pp. 593–606, https://doi.org/10.1093/oxfordhb/9780190277352.013.46.

Woodfin, W. T. (2012). *The Embodied Icon: Liturgical Vestments and Sacramental Power in Byzantium*. Oxford: Oxford University Press.

Woodfin, W. T. (2010). Celestial Hierarchies and Earthly Hierarchies in the Art of the Byzantine Church. In P. Stephenson, ed., *The Byzantine World*. London: Routledge, pp. 303–319.

Woodfin, W. T. (2004). Liturgical Textiles. In H. Evans, ed., *Byzantium: Faith and Power (1261-1557)*. New York: The Metropolitan Museum of Art, pp. 295–323.

Woodward Wendelken, R. (2014). Wefts and Worms: The Spread of Sericulture and Silk Weaving in the West before 1300. In R. Netherton and G. Owen-Crocker, *Medieval Clothing and Textiles*. Woodbridge: Boydell Press, pp. 59–77.

Wouters, J. (1995). Dye Analysis in a Broad Perspective: A Study of 3rd- to 10th-Century Coptic Textiles from Belgian Private Collections. *Dyes in History and Archaeology*, **13**, 38–45.

Xu, J. (2019). The Funerary Couch of An Jia and the Art of Sogdian Immigrants in Sixth-Century China. *The Burlington Magazine*, **10**, 820–829.

Yarza Luaces, J. (1999). Un cycle de fresques romanes dans la paroisse de Santa María de Taüll. *Les cahiers de Saint-Michel de Cuxa*, **30**, 121–140.

Zhao, F., S. Sardjono, and C. Buckley (2019). *A World of Looms: Weaving Technology and Textile Arts*. Hangzhou: Zhejiang University Press.

Acknowledgments

We thank the Global Middle Ages editors, Gerry Heng and Susan Noakes, for the invitation to participate in this new series and to combine our shared expertise in one study. Their feedback, as well as the comments of our anonymous reviewers, improved and sharpened our text. We thank Michele Mazeris in the Visual Resources Collection of the Department of Art & Archaeology at Princeton University for her help clearing image rights, and are grateful to the institutions that granted those rights or provide open-access images of the objects in their collections. Funding for images came from the Barr Ferree Foundation Fund, Department of Art & Archaeology, Princeton University. For help and suggestions while working on this project, we are grateful to Jennifer Ball, Maria Cristina Carile, Anna Kelley, Amanda Luyster, and Pamela A. Patton. We thank Liz Friend-Smith, Adam Hooper, Atifa Jiwa, and Priya Samidurai of Cambridge University Press for their hard work on this Element.

We dedicate this work to our children, Aline, Anna, Karel, Mateo and Oliver, who were born and grew alongside us as we read, thought, discussed, and wrote this Element.

Cambridge Elements ≡

The Global Middle Ages

Geraldine Heng
University of Texas at Austin

Geraldine Heng is Perceval Professor of English and Comparative Literature at the University of Texas, Austin. She is the author of *The Invention of Race in the European Middle Ages* (2018) and *England and the Jews: How Religion and Violence Created the First Racial State in the West* (2018), both published by Cambridge University Press, as well as *Empire of Magic: Medieval Romance and the Politics of Cultural Fantasy* (2003, Columbia). She is the editor of *Teaching the Global Middle Ages* (2022, MLA), coedits the University of Pennsylvania Press series, RaceB4Race: Critical Studies of the Premodern, and is working on a new book, Early Globalisms: The Interconnected World, 500–1500 CE. Originally from Singapore, Heng is a Fellow of the Medieval Academy of America, a member of the Medievalists of Color, and Founder and Co-director, with Susan Noakes, of the Global Middle Ages Project: www.globalmiddleages.org.

Susan Noakes
University of Minnesota, Twin Cities

Susan Noakes is Professor and Chair of French and Italian at the University of Minnesota, Twin Cities. From 2002 to 2008 she was Director of the Center for Medieval Studies; she has also served as Director of Italian Studies, Director of the Center for Advanced Feminist Studies, and Associate Dean for Faculty in the College of Liberal Arts. Her publications include *The Comparative Perspective on Literature: Essays in Theory and Practice* (co-edited with Clayton Koelb, Cornell, 1988) and *Timely Reading: Between Exegesis and Interpretation* (Cornell, 1988), along with many articles and critical editions in several areas of French, Italian, and neo-Latin Studies. She is the Founder and Co-director, with Geraldine Heng, of the Global Middle Ages Project: www.globalmiddleages.org.

About the Series

Elements in the Global Middle Ages is a series of concise studies that introduce researchers and instructors to an uncentered, interconnected world, c. 500–1500 CE. Individual Elements focus on the globe's geographic zones, its natural and built environments, its cultures, societies, arts, technologies, peoples, ecosystems, and lifeworlds.

Cambridge Elements ≡

The Global Middle Ages